Everything New Teachers Need to Know But Are Afraid to Ask

Grad programs in education teach you theory and pedagogy, but where do you learn the logistics of your new teaching role? In this unique book, Amber Chandler comes to the rescue as your friendly but honest mentor. She provides answers on everything new teachers need to know but are afraid to ask, such as how to build knowledge about the school's culture, nurture relationships with colleagues and superiors, use social media appropriately, navigate various faculty and parent meetings, handle conflicts, and more. Unlike new teacher books focused on instruction, this one helps you with everyday logistics and teacher life. Each chapter is written in a conversational tone with loads of practical advice to support you in your first year. Each chapter also contains a Mentoring Moments reflection section, so you can discuss the book with your school mentor or in new-teacher induction programs.

Amber Chandler is a National Board Certified middle school English language arts (ELA) teacher in Hamburg, New York, and an adjunct professor at Canisius College in Buffalo, New York. No matter which level Chandler is teaching, the goal is always the same: to enable students to take charge of their own learning. Chandler's website, flexibleclass.com, has many resources to support teachers, and she regularly updates lessons and provides links to her webinars. Follow her on Twitter @MsAmberChandler and check out over 300 of her free resources on ShareMyLesson.com.

Everything New Teachers Need to Know But Are Afraid to Ask

An Honest Guide to the Nuts and Bolts of Your First Job

Amber Chandler

Routledge
Taylor & Francis Group

NEW YORK AND LONDON

Designed cover image: © Getty Images

First published 2024
by Routledge
605 Third Avenue, New York, NY 10158

and by Routledge
4 Park Square, Milton Park, Abingdon, Oxon, OX14 4RN

Routledge is an imprint of the Taylor & Francis Group, an informa business

© 2024 Amber Chandler

ISBN: 978-1-032-43154-3 (hbk)
ISBN: 978-1-032-43124-6 (pbk)
ISBN: 978-1-003-36592-1 (ebk)

DOI: 10.4324/9781003365921

Typeset in Palatino
by codeMantra

Contents

Meet the author

Amber Chandler is a National Board Certified middle school ELA teacher in Hamburg, New York, with a master's degree in Literature, as well as a School District Leader certification. She was the 2018 AMLE Educator of the Year and the 2022 New York State Teacher of the Year finalist. Amber has enjoyed a wide variety of teaching opportunities. Amber is an 8th grade middle school ELA teacher, as well as an adjunct professor at Canisius College. No matter which level Amber is teaching, the goal is always the same: engage students to take charge of their own learning.

Amber's blogs and articles have appeared in MiddleWeb, ShareMyLesson, Getting Smart, ASCD's "Ideas From the Field," Mom's Rising, The EdVocate, *AMLE Magazine*, as well as *New York Teacher*. Amber's blogs and webinars for AFT's ShareMyLesson have repeatedly been in the top of the year, and several in the top five of the decade. Amber enjoys speaking about student engagement, Project Based Learning, and SEL, at AFT TEACH, the AMLE annual conference, and Learning and the Brain conferences.

Amber was chosen from a nationwide search as one of a handful of panelists for Fordham's "Evaluating the Content and Quality of Next Generation Assessments" to evaluate how state assessments compare in their ability to assess Common Core Standards. She's also served as a School Review Team member, offering her observations and expertise, particularly in the area of Project Based Learning.

Amber is an SEL consultant for Capstone Publisher's "My Spectacular Self" series, as well as for the GoPebble! Division. She provides SEL questions for student engagement, as well as offers developmentally appropriate advice to parents.

Amber is an active AFT member as a ShareMyLesson Partner and participant in the Resource and Materials Development at the Summer Educators Academy. Amber recently served on NYSUT's "Future Forward Taskforce" as a voice for SEL initiatives as schools return to in-person, post-pandemic instruction. She serves as the president for her local, Frontier Central Teachers Association.

Amber's website, flexibleclass.com, has many resources to support teachers, and she regularly updates lessons and provides links to her webinars. Follow her on Twitter @MsAmberChandler and check out over 300 of her free resources on ShareMyLesson.com.

Foreword

I taught at my first school for months before realizing I was storing my lunch in the uncool fridge.

By this, I don't mean a fridge that ran too warm or didn't keep food chilled enough. No, I mean a fridge no one else used. There was another fridge in an entirely different room most staff used instead. I actually had no idea that fridge even existed until I followed a staff member into that room one day to join them for lunch and realized, aha, *this* is the fridge everyone uses.

I left college well prepared for the actual work of teaching—classroom management, lesson planning, pedagogy, philosophies of education, and discipline. But no amount of collegiate preparation could have tipped me off about the dorky fridge scenario.

We know we're losing new teachers within the first five years of their entrance to the classroom at an alarming—and unsustainable—rate. Among the commonly purported solutions to this problem, such as increasing pay and strengthening teacher preparatory programs, is mentorship. Many schools and districts have new employee mentorship structures, and though some are robust and effective, many remain little more than obedient completion of a compulsory process, lacking impactful mentor/mentee relationships. My own experience as a mentee fell somewhere between. My mentor was a PE teacher, and though she was very kind to me and did a great job orienting me to the district's specific practices, like data binders and tracking attendance and work completion, her experience as a PE teacher didn't align to my newbie experiences in the world of middle school special education. I struggled to get my footing in my new position, and topics like what fridge to store my lunch in or where I could get more post-it notes when I ran out never came up—nor would I have even known to ask about such things.

I needed a work mom.

In this book, Amber offers to be just that. In her engaging, highly conversational writing style, Amber serves as your "work mom," walking you through the logistics of entering a new teaching job, from selecting a health insurance policy to navigating staff parking lot politics and more. Structured with "Mentoring Moments" at the end of each chapter, Amber provides practical guidance for mentee/mentor partnerships. Or, if you don't have access to a strong mentor, you can use Amber's questions and prompts to help you think it all through.

In a session on the rate of loss of new teachers at SXSWedu in March of 2023, JoLisa Hoover of Raise Your Hand Texas said, "When we see that number, that's a tally of broken dreams." Addressing the teacher shortage will be no small task. But to quote the emperor in Disney's animated movie *Mulan*, "A single grain of rice can tip the scale. One man may be the difference between victory and defeat." Amber has taken action, doing her part to tangibly and thoughtfully support new teachers. I'm quite confident Amber's grain of rice will have an effective and lasting impact on those who read this book, hopefully empowering a few more new teachers to get to live out their dreams, and maybe reigniting hope and passion for a few veteran teacher mentors as well.

—Katie Powell, Educator, Author, and
Director of Middle Level Programs at AMLE

A letter to readers

Dear Reader,

Chances are if you are reading this book, you are a mentor teacher or a newer teacher (whether to the profession or to a new district/school setting). Last year was my first year in a new district and I was lucky enough to have Amber as my mentor. I'm not sure how much I believe in fate, but when it came to being paired with Amber as my mentor, I genuinely believe it was. Not only was Amber in my content area, ELA, but she also is the president of the Teachers' Association for our district. As far as mentors go, I hit the jackpot. Luckily for me, and maybe not so lucky for Amber, my classroom was situated right down the hallway where I could bother her whenever I wanted.

Mornings usually started, and still start, with a stop in Amber's room with basic questions like: How was your weekend? Where can I print to? Does wearing leggings as pants make me look unprofessional? Does this situation qualify as a sick day or personal day? A parent just friend requested me on social media, what do I do? But sometimes they started with more complex questions: This situation made me uncomfortable, where do I go from here? Do I need to call CPS? Did I handle this situation correctly, if not, how do I fix it? It got to the point where one day I just started calling Amber my work mom because she seemed to have the answers and advice that only a real mom can give.

Starting a new job is never easy, but to be a new teacher? Sometimes it feels like an impossible task. You're trying to win over administrators, coworkers, parents, and most importantly, the students, all while learning the ins and outs of a new work environment. This is why I wish I had Amber and *Everything New Teachers Need to Know but Are Afraid to Ask: An Honest Guide to the Nuts and Bolts of Your First Job* when I first started teaching.

However, I am five years into my career and still can use this book as a guide when Amber is too busy, which, miraculously despite her many hats, she still seems to make time for me.

By writing this book, Amber has made time for not just me, but for all teachers that need a guiding hand. Asking for help isn't always easy, but asking your mom for advice? It has never been easier.

Remember, moms really do know best, and in this case, Amber has your back.

Sincerely,
Nicole Coolican

Photo of Nicole Coolican with the author, Amber Chandler.

Introduction

Pretty much everyone has heard of the book *What to Expect When You're Expecting*. After reading it from cover to cover many times, and consulting it often when we had our first child, my husband and I joked that we needed to write a book called *Well, No One Warned Us About That*. Don't get me wrong, we loved the *What to Expect* series, but we felt there needed to be a little more casual and humorous version that might make us feel better about all we didn't know. We never wrote that book (and maybe we should!), but I know that we often felt so ridiculous about what we didn't know, and we truly didn't have anywhere to turn.

Can I leave our three month old on the floor while I run to the other room? How does anyone take a shower? Do I have to wear my baby? Why do I feel like putting my baby in a crib is like sentencing her to prison? Why is my three-year old pooping on the floor every time I nurse the baby? How do I introduce the dog and cat to our baby? What if she won't eat anything healthy? Now, hopefully those of you who are parents or aunts and uncles realize that these are not, in fact, stupid questions. They are perfectly reasonable for two very carefree adults who suddenly had a human life to be responsible for all the time. We were shocked that any baby made it to adulthood given how little we seemed to know. I'm happy to report that we have two teenagers now, and there is not a book for that either, and we certainly wish there was! We are doing ok by relying on our instincts and asking lots of questions.

This book hopes to be about all the things that weren't on the syllabus as you learned to be a teacher, but are important and relevant questions that somehow are being overlooked. Every district is going to be different. Every school, for that matter, is going to have its own unwritten rules, culture, climate, and organizational structure. However, there are some universal pieces of advice that I would have loved to have gotten at 22 or 23. I've mentored teachers for two decades, and my mentees always have great questions and we are often baffled, shaking our heads, frequently feeling that same wonderment as my husband and I did: *Well, No One Warned Me about That!*

As I always feel when beginning a book, I have a strong need to explain why you should listen to me! I've been teaching for 22 years and mentored over a dozen teachers. I teach courses at Canisius College to teachers-to-be. I'm the president of our Teachers' union, and I am very involved with helping our new teachers get acclimated and becoming successful. The truth is, teachers are given a whole lot of theory, a little bit of practice, and then are given not one, but dozens of children! Then, they are expected to also navigate healthcare, so many meetings, committees, paperwork, and institutional knowledge that seems impossible to decipher.

I'd love for mentor teachers to share this book with those new teachers, but I know that it is often left to new teachers to look for help on their own. This book, I hope, will help answer the questions that weren't on the syllabus, the questions that no one else seems to be asking, and frankly, a bunch of questions that you might not even know to ask. My daughter is a senior, and she's going to college next year to be a teacher. It is helpful for me to frame this book by thinking, what would she need to know? How can I protect her interests?

I want to protect your interests as well. Think of me as your "Work Mom," as my current mentee, Nicole, described me. After getting over the shock that I could, indeed, be the mom of this full-grown woman, I have to admit, I was honored. Being a "Work Mom" is an amazing way to give back to the profession that has given me so much. The truth is *we need you*. As a veteran teacher, I believe that it is our obligation to take the "newbies" under our wings. We have so much to learn from you, but, as you read this book, you'll see that oftentimes experience is truly the best teacher and that's the one thing you can't rush. I hope you find this book helpful, a little but humorous, and a way to ease some of the stress of perpetually figuring out this amazing (and terrifying) career. Now, drink some water, get a good night's sleep, and remember tomorrow is a new day.

Fondly,

Your Work Mom

1

You're hired. Now what?

Finally. You've waited your whole life to have your own class-room. You have Pinterest boards for everything from class-room activities to decorations, and your parents' basement is overflowing with dollar store finds that you just had to stock up on. Your wardrobe has had an official makeover, and you are ready for your first day in the classroom. The wait is finally over. This all sounds ideal until you are sweating in an overstuffed boardroom with other equally eager new teachers experiencing "orientation." As anyone who has lived to tell the tale will tell you, "orientation" can be a bit, well, *disorienting*.

Information is being fired so quickly that your head is swimming. There's so many decisions. You are petrified that somehow you'll mess this up before you start, yet your mind will not stay focused because you just want to get to your classroom. This is what it feels like when you're hired. After the elation, the celebration, and the planning, there's a distinct "now what" that settles in, and that is exactly the point of this book—to lay out some of the choices that you have, some of the things that might not have occurred to you, and some friendly "work mom" advice that might save you from the near-disasters that I've lived through myself and let you in on some of the conversations I've had with the dozen teachers I've mentored over the years.

But first, a story. In April of 1999, I was student teaching at Portsmouth High School in New Hampshire. I got married over spring break, as teachers often do (and have babies then

DOI: 10.4324/9781003365921-1

too—more on that later). In May, I am hired by the same district in a very unceremonious way. I simply got a call to go to the superintendents' office and walked out 20 minutes later with the job. It was all a sort of surreal dream. Summer came and went, and I prepared and planned, and was so ready! I'd finally gotten around to changing my name right before school started and doing all the "married lady" things like setting up my bank account, getting those cute little return address stickers, and writing thank-you notes for all of our wedding gifts.

Except I forgot a very big "married lady" thing. I forgot to tell the district that I had changed my name from Crawford to Chandler. My first paycheck—an actual check—was delivered to my school mailbox. I opened it up, relieved that I was finally going to be paid. Rent was due. I wanted new clothes for school. My gas tank was nearing empty. I drove to the bank to deposit the check and was met with catastrophic news. The bank could not cash my check. In my "married lady" hurry, I'd opened the account with my new name, and I didn't even provide a maiden name in the space they'd provided. The bank told me I had to notify my employer, have them cut a new check, and they needed to change my name or I'd have tax issues too.

I didn't make it to my car before I was crying, hoping that I had enough gas to get to my central office. It was Friday at 4:00 pm. This used to mean things—before constant communication was conceived, banks had open and closed hours and there was no such thing as scanning a check with your phone to deposit it. Banks were closed on weekends. After my first two weeks, I was going to have no money, and, apparently, tax issues! My landlord actually came around to our apartment on Saturday mornings, and without this check, we wouldn't have enough to cover it.

What it meant was that I needed to get someone at the central office to change my name AND cut me a check within the hour. If you've been involved in a school district for even a few short weeks, you may have already guessed that this was impossible. There are processes for these important "married lady" things. Except, I was 24 years old, and this was my first real job, and I had no idea what I was doing. I explained my plight to the superintendents' secretary, who was definitely not even the right person to appeal to. I soon learned that I needed to go to personnel and to payroll to make the necessary changes. Then, I heard this terrifying sentence: "If you hurry up and do this by Monday, they'll be able to just double up your checks for the next payday."

I've blocked a bunch of the following 20 minutes out of my head until I write this now, but I'll share my raw, embarrassing, and *completely understandable* meltdown here. I burst into tears. I started ugly crying, laying my life story out for this kindly secretary. She offered me tissues and tea, both of which I took. An older man came around the corner, and nodded to me.

"Would you mind coming into my office for a minute," he asked. I'll be completely honest here. I thought I was in trouble with this man—whomever he was—for, as my mama would say, "pitching a fit" in the middle of a place of business.

I started apologizing. He didn't engage with me. He simply said, "It seems you have found yourself in a predicament," pronouncing it "predictament." He took a big ledger and checkbook out of the drawer. He asked me for my name, and for me to give him the check please. I did. It was useless to me anyway.

He looked at the total and wrote a check for that amount. He told me to fix the problem on Monday by changing my name and providing payroll with the update. He stood up, started putting on his brown trench coat and hat, and indicated that I should leave too.

I'm embarrassed to say that I have no idea who this man was. He must have been a business director, or treasurer, or an assistant superintendent because he wrote a check from the district. Knowing all I know now, I am guessing that he used some sort of flexible budget line to write the check, and he would notify payroll the following week. To this day, I don't know who this was. (Also, note to my rookie self, you should ALWAYS follow up with a thank you when anyone in the district goes out of their way to help you!)

Why do I share this embarrassing story? Because the reason I am writing this book is to do everything in my power to prevent you from making the "rookie mistakes" that can at the very least sap your energy, most definitely make you question yourself, and at worst truly mess up your career. There are simply too many decisions and scenarios that are unique to expect that I'll cover them all, but I'll try to cover the most prevalent ones.

In this chapter, we will focus on the month immediately after you are hired. This is the point in time when tricky decisions are being made, and you simply don't know what you don't know. *Here we go—you're hired. Now what?*

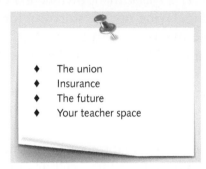

- ◆ The union
- ◆ Insurance
- ◆ The future
- ◆ Your teacher space

The union

Full disclosure here. I'm proudly serving my third term as the president of a teacher's union, involved pretty heavily with my state and even the national teachers' union. But, that wasn't always the case, and when I first started out, I had no idea if I should join the union or not. For some, this isn't even an option, but the sheer largesse of the union is noteworthy. During the pandemic, it was the American Federation of Teachers who provided a roadmap for a safe return to school months before anyone else was willing to commit to a plan. Politics aside, joining the union is a practical decision, and it will help to know how most work.

The primary role of a teachers' union is to negotiate the teachers' contract which details your obligations, your rate of pay, your work day, your opportunities to earn additional money (like coaching or supervising detention), as well as determine the number of sick days that you have. Additionally, the union negotiates with the district to determine how many days you receive for bereavement of a family member, ways that you can expect to be treated by administrators, and your retirement incentives and benefits. Your union works to support teachers from the beginning of their career all the way into retirement. These are the proactive things your union would do for you.

There are also ways that your union must react *with* you and sometimes *for* you. One of the scariest events that can ever happen to a teacher is to face a disciplinary investigation or worse yet, disciplinary action. Without a union, each teacher is on their own. When you join a union, you are afforded representation—a union representative—to be present when you are being questioned in a disciplinary situation to protect your best interests. If you think that you are a "cookie cutter, goody goody, rule follower teacher," and this will never happen to you, let me warn you: if you teach long enough, you likely will. Most things like this are easily resolved without consequence. Many have minor repercussions. A handful have major, life-altering results.

No one is perfect. Sometimes you will do things that could create problems for yourself simply because you didn't know what to do. Scenario: you are very sick. You wake up with your alarm, hit snooze. You took Nyquil in the middle of the night, and you are in a fog. Eventually, you turn the alarm off. When you finally awake, you know that you have screwed up big time. Unintentionally, you have not shown up for work. Your students were unsupervised until it was reported. Your phone has three messages. One from the school secretary, one from your best teacher friend, and another from your principal.

Many of you might be hoping that I'll tell you exactly what you should do in this case, but I can't. But, a union representative will know the parameters of your contract, what you were supposed to have done, who you need to talk to and in what manner. The union representative will likely be a knowledgeable veteran teacher who has experienced something like this before or known someone who has. Most importantly, if you are in real trouble, they will have access as a part of their union affiliation to the state and national teachers' union resources. At the least, you are going to be having some really uncomfortable conversations. At the worst, this could be cause for an untenured teacher to be dismissed.

Some states provide no protection for teachers who haven't reached tenure yet. Technically, in my state and many others, administration can fire an untenured teacher without a hearing and without a burden of proof. According to "Terminating a Tenured Versus Non-Tenured Employee Working at a Public or Charter School," guidance on the Hanson Niemann and Wright website in March of 2022,

> Going through the process of dismissing a teacher who has tenure can be difficult, particularly if the school is trying to prove that a teacher was inefficient or engaged in conduct unbecoming to the school. When it comes to non-tenured employees, schools have more flexibility and can terminate the employee on any basis they feel is appropriate.

In these complicated times, tenure is a saving grace from the increasingly angry mob that often attacks teachers and what we do. Without unions, there would be no tenure, and without tenure, there is no protection.

I know this is a hot-button political issue. There's no doubt that strong opinions are out there, and one of those with a different opinion lives in my house! His argument is that unions protect bad teachers. My argument is that unfortunately, good teachers—and especially life-alteringly influential and committed teachers—need protections, particularly in the current climate. No matter your opinion, you should learn your contract inside and out. It is important to understand that even if you are not a member, the contract is still the document the district will follow in how it treats you and the expectations it has for you. Contracts are often quite picky, and dictate much of the daily life of a teacher, and being familiar with it would benefit members and non-members alike.

Insurance

Sometime during that sweaty orientation, a person, usually dressed in a suit, is going to come and explain your health insurance options to you. Every year, one of my roles as president is to go to orientation and make the pitch for the teachers to join the union. After my spiel, I always say, "I've been a teacher in the district for two decades. What questions do you have about anything you've heard today? Not just from me, but from your orientation." Without exception, the biggest question is "do I take the high deductible or low deductible health insurance" and "can I just stay on my parents' health insurance?" Admittedly, I didn't know the answers to these questions off the top of my head, but I did my homework to share with my members, and here's what I found.

In the United States, high deductible insurance policies have lower premiums (the part you have to pay whether you use your insurance or not), with higher deductibles. If you have a low premium, you will have to have a high deductible, which varies from policy to policy. According to healthcare.gov, "For 2022, the IRS defines a high deductible health plan as any plan with a deductible of at least $1400 for an individual or $2800 for a family." The site also explains, "A high deductible plan (HDHP can be combined with a health savings account (HSA), allowing you to pay for certain medical expenses with money free from federal taxes." If you are feeling even more confused, you aren't alone. I won't even tell you how little I knew about insurance when I first started teaching. However, the choices you make can have big implications.

Only you know the extent of your healthcare needs, so this is a deeply personal decision. There are a few things to consider. First, is your age and your parents' willingness to allow you to remain on their insurance. The good news is that if you are covered by your parents' plan, you can stay on it until you are 26, even if you have a job (and even if you get married or have a child of your own). This can vary by state, but this is the general rule. If your parents are willing to absorb the cost, or allow you to pay them, this is a good choice. However, if you do not live in the same state or even part of the state, you might have issues finding in-plan doctors. Some plans allow for this, but others are stricter. You'll need to discuss the pros and cons with your parents.

If you have any tricky health condition that requires more constant care, a high deductible plan is probably not for you unless you have a health savings account (HSA). Even if you are a relatively healthy young person, we are living in complicated times when it comes to healthcare. For example, many of the common ailments that are a simply a part of working in schools with all the germy kiddos—colds, strep, bronchitis—all have similar symptoms of Covid, and you might be required to take a test in order to return to work after exhibiting those symptoms. That can happen multiple times in a year!

The really great news is that teachers typically have what my husband calls the "Cadillac health plan." For a time, he worked for an insurance provider, and my insurance as a teacher was still more inclusive and less expensive than what he was offered. Unionized school districts typically have better insurance since it is a negotiated benefit. Each district will have a liaison who works directly with the insurance company. You can request to speak to the liaison who will be able to help you understand what options you have and more importantly be able to give you the name of their contact or a real person to speak with.

Insurance is ultimately a way to protect yourself against potential costs associated with healthcare. You could be super healthy and really lucky, and still pay your premiums, yet never go to the doctor for an entire year, feeling that you have wasted your money. As your work mom for a moment, I'd like to remind you of a few key facts though. Anecdotally, most teachers will be sick by Thanksgiving. The amount of germs that you live with, the wear and tear on your immune system, and the general stress of teaching can do a number on you.

Let's assume that you have mega defenses in your young and healthy body. What about your mental health though? As a mental health advocate, I'll nudge you toward therapy the first time you walk into my classroom near tears. I simply believe that an outside, unbiased, professional can help anyone deal with their lives. MentalHealthAmerica.org, in their article, "Teachers: Protecting Your Mental Health," explains, "According to several studies and reports, teaching is one of the most stressful jobs in the country," going on to cite The American Federation of

Teachers' 2017 Educator Quality of Work Life Survey that found that "61 percent of teachers said their jobs were always or often stressful—more than double the rate of non-teaching working adults—and 58 percent said they had poor mental health due to stress levels." This was pre-Covid, so you can imagine which direction these numbers are trending now.

I know that this is not the most exciting thing in the world to talk about, but there is nothing worse than being unprepared when it comes to your physical and mental well-being. It doesn't matter so much which choice you choose here: stay on your parents' plan, high deductible with lower premiums, or low deductible with higher premiums. What matters is that you have thoughtfully considered what is best for your situation, rather than ask the person sitting next to you what they are doing. I did that. I am not joking. My first year, I asked what the other newly hired teacher next to me was going to do about their health insurance, and when they told me, I just did the same thing. It sounded right. Incidentally, it was a horrible decision, since I LEFT MY HUSBAND OFF!!! Luckily, when I got home, my husband looked over everything and caught the "mistake." I was able to make a change before the paperwork was filed, but you don't always get that lucky. What was I thinking? *I wasn't.* It's that simple. I wasn't used to being married yet, and I simply forgot. Don't be me. Remember if you are married!

In all seriousness, this is a really important part of being hired, and I greatly appreciate my health insurance. With two kids, the husband I forgot that first week I was hired, and myself, health insurance is the single most important benefit of being a teacher. By all means, chat with other employees, talk to your parents, set up a meeting with the healthcare liaison if you have questions, and read the plan to see what benefits are offered. I mention this last bit because to this day I spend time pointing out to new and not-so-new hires that benefits like discounted gym memberships, massage, consultations with nutritionists, and even discounts on orthotics and running shoes can be a part of a plan but often go unnoticed. I've taken to signing my emails, "Stay Well," and if that doesn't tell you I'm turning 50, I don't know what does! Take care of yourself.

The future

I'm going to share two brief stories about managing money. The first is really crucial in the short term. Many districts offer a 21 pay and a 26 pay option. This means that you'll either receive 21 paychecks or 26 paychecks. There are tax implications, but that has never been the deciding factor for me. Understand this: if you choose 21 paychecks, **YOU WILL NOT GET PAID IN THE SUMMER**. I am yelling this, which is why it is all capitalized and bolded. Every single year there is a new teacher who misses this key detail and finds themselves with rent due and no more checks coming in. Sure, their paychecks during the school year were a little bigger, but until you have your life figured out, I'd opt for 26 pays. This way, even if you don't land a summer job, you will have money for over the summer. Almost all new teachers, and many veteran ones, work over the summer, but the back up plan of checks rolling in can't be beat. To this day, I always pick 26 paychecks, since it is really hard to know what summer will look like. Will I want to work or will I need a break? I'm sure there's some financial advisor-ish person reading this who will tell you the benefits of the 21 pays. Self-discipline could allow you to save for the summer and have 21 pays, but I myself like the sure thing.

If you are thinking longer term, most districts will offer you a 403B, a way to save money with the taxes deferred until you spend the money. Sometimes employers will also make matching contributions. Small contributions now can add up. There are many calculators online which will tell you how much money you'll have upon retirement. Of all the advice I'll try to give you in this book, the hardest to understand as a young person is that one day you'll be very concerned with some of the most boring topics on the planet! I remember being in high school and my dad getting a new job and trying to explain to me his "deferred compensation plan," and his excitement was incomprehensible to me at the time. Now, I know that his "deferred compensation plan" helped pay for my wedding! Again, this falls into the category of "you don't know what you don't know." I wish that I had someone who had forced me to contribute to my 403b

20 years ago. I'm not even going to do the calculator because it would sicken me, so humor your work mom and put even $20 a paycheck in!

Your teacher space

Soon after those disorienting orientation days, you'll go to meet with your principal and get settled into your scheduled. There is nothing that breeds panic more than a new and vulnerable teacher heading to their building after orientation to find out that they are "on a cart" or that they will be "traveling." This happens more than it should, for sure, but it is crucial that you hear me on this point: *do not freak out*. If you have to go sit in your car and cry, do that. If you have to call your real mom and complain, do so. Do not, I repeat, do not be rude to anyone. Do not complain about the person who is in "your" room, and don't act like the room was owed to you. Of course you should know if you have a classroom or if you are traveling, but that was a question that you could have asked in the interview. Of course, you wouldn't think of that since everyone on television and the movies who teaches has their own beautiful, Pinterest-worthy rooms.

In real life, there are sometimes shortages of space. There are often a lot of personal politics around rooms—things that have nothing to do with you! Don't take it personally, and don't look at it as an indication of anything other than what it is: lack of space. This is an area where administrators mostly follow seniority. For example, a teacher can teach at a school for five years, go on maternity leave, and then return the very same year you are supposed to get "her" room. The majority of the time, she will get her room back, and you'll end up paying your dues on a cart, or in my case, with a backpack.

It had never occurred to me that you could even be a teacher without a room—which goes to show you how much I'd thought about this, since if you look around a school, some of the greatest teachers don't have their own room. For example, many special education teachers "push in" to classrooms, and they are certainly some of the best teachers among us. I had moved from New Hampshire, where I was an AP Literature teacher to mostly seniors, where I had a retro, funky Sesame Street themed room. When I reported to my principal at the middle school in New York, and I was told that I'd be in five different classrooms, I thought seriously about quitting. Again, not my brightest move, but luckily my husband gave me a pep talk, and I stuck it out.

Most teachers who travel have a cart to lug all their stuff around. I was on two different floors, and my classrooms were too far apart to try to navigate an elevator, so I was relegated to a backpack. I was more sad about this fact than I should admit, but in retrospect, traveling had a really great silver lining. Teaching is very isolating, and as a new teacher to a building, it is easy to hide in your room and work yourself silly. However, I had to teach in other people's rooms, and I got to know lots of teachers who I'd never have met otherwise.

With that being said, there are a few rules to live by if you are traveling and forced to teach in someone else's space.

First, respect their stuff. Do not erase what they have written. Don't use their supplies. Don't take it for granted that they want you there—they probably don't. Most teachers will be amiable—and as a union president I really emphasize that we are "in this together," but once you have a room, you'll want to be in it! Most teachers contractually have to leave the room if another teacher is teaching in their room, but many won't want to. Their stuff is there! But, what is worse than having another teacher—an experienced one at that—be there, watching you teach? I get it.

Here's my practical advice, and it is based on reality, not what *should* be. Of course, teachers *should* vacate the room when you teach. Of course, they *should* provide you with space in the room for your materials or to show student work. Of course, they *should* leave space on the board for you (Yes, I know, most are not using a chalkboard, but you get the gist.) How can you navigate this scenario, all while mourning the fact that you thought you were going to have your own space?

The short answer is "very carefully." The longer answer is that there is probably nothing more important than the relationships you build with your co-workers. If you can approach the situation with an accurate read on the circumstance and try to take the "I" out of all of your phrasing, it will help. For example, as you introduce yourself, it is probably not a good idea to say "I'm supposed to have this room." For teachers who've already paid their dues and finally have a room, hearing this from a person who doesn't even know where the bathroom is, much less how things work in the building, is a bit off putting. Instead, "My schedule says that I'm teaching in your room period 2. I'm really sorry about that" goes a long way toward recognizing the awkward, or at least potentially awkward, situations.

You might be asking yourself why the onus to be the "bigger person" comes to you versus someone who isn't freaking out, scared to death, and really worried how to do all of this. I'm not going to say it is fair, but I will say that I've watched several new teachers really struggle because they came across as entitled. Demanding, shouting, crying, or interrogating anyone—especially the person who you are going to share a room with—is simply a bad idea. The best approach is humility, the recognition that you've been thrown into a weird situation, and if you can look at it as a learning experience or a potential work BFF or work mom, then the experience can be bearable.

From a practical standpoint, my backpack was filled with the necessities: pencils, paper, a notebook, candy, pens, stickers, deodorant (I walked a long way!), water, and a jump drive. I'm jump drive level old. You'll probably have a computer or be able to sign into Google Classroom or Microsoft Teams. My husband, who was a godsend with my busted ego who wanted her own room to decorate really cute, reminded me that time in the halls with kiddos would be time I could talk with them. I would get to meet new people. I could commiserate with late kiddos. All true, but it still was really hard.

The second year, I had my own classroom, and things went back to what I really expected. However, and this is the key, I now offer my room to new teachers, give them snacks, leave a space for them in my classroom, and try to be the dream roommate. I leave the room when they are teaching. I don't repeat anything that I hear, and I sure as heck don't observe since that isn't my job. So, as you live the life of a new teacher, remember the lessons of those first days and become the person you needed. You'll get through those first few months, and sleep through Thanksgiving, just like all of us before you!

Mentoring moment

After reading this chapter, use these questions to help you be intentional about your decisions and actions. Find a mentor (either assigned or found), grab a cup of coffee, and talk over these questions. Be sure to find out how your mentor has handled these situations!

1. What kind of healthcare is offered by the district? Does it makes sense to get it now, or should you stay on your parent's policy? Do the math!
2. Who is the union president in your district? If you have second thoughts, be sure to reach out to get more information to make an informed decision.
3. What is your teaching space? If it is a classroom, check the schedule because often you'll have a teacher coming in during your free period. Think about how you'd want to be treated and make them welcome. If you are a teacher who must travel to different classrooms, make sure you introduce yourself. Make a plan with your mentor about how you'll handle this situation.

Resources

"Things to Know Before Picking a Health Insurance Plan." *HealthCare.gov*, https://www.healthcare.gov/choose-a-plan/comparing-plans/.

Glover, Lacie, and Kate Ashford. "How to Choose Health Insurance: Your Step-by-Step Guide." *NerdWallet*, https://www.nerdwallet.com/article/health/choose-health-insurance.

Meador, Derrick. "Pros and Cons of Joining a Teachers Union." *ThoughtCo*, 27 Aug. 2020, thoughtco.com/weighing-the-decision-to-join-a-teachers-union-3194787.

2

The social (media) dilemma

When it comes to advice for new teachers, I don't think there's a topic that veteran teachers disagree about more than social media. I'm going to present you with the views of the polar ends with the understanding that many people fall somewhere on the continuum. At one end, social media causes drama, jealousy, and lasting damage to inexperienced teachers' careers. At the other end, social media allows a community of educators to unite, and share materials and insights and provides a positive climate for those whose IRL (in real life) school might not be as encouraging. As I write this, I am excitedly watching my Twitter feed because I will soon have 5000 followers, so you can guess which pole I gravitate toward.

Let's start though with a cautionary tale since that is really important information, even for social media enthusiasts like myself. This is what I'll call an "in the weeds" story, but that is how social media misunderstandings often go. I mention this story in the second edition of *The Flexible SEL Classroom*, but I'd like to dissect it a bit more here to make the dangers of social media on your reputation, mental health, and potentially your career crystal clear.

Upon returning from the pandemic, I decided to go old school and begin with a novel that I thought would capture my 8th graders' imaginations. I poked around, and found copies of *The Pigman*, the Paul Zindel 1968 classic. I had loved this book when I was a teen, and thought it was charming and loved the

DOI: 10.4324/9781003365921-2

emphasis on psychology and family dynamics. School started, and we jumped right in. I shared a digital notebook with all of our lessons on the novel to my students, posted it on my website for families to see, and tweeted about it. This is what I always do. I like to be 100% transparent, and in all honesty, it keeps me on my toes knowing that anyone can see what we are doing in class. Maybe it is just me, but when I know I have a larger audience, I'm a bit more careful that everything is just perfect.

The first piece of important information to this story is that this is the second week of school. I'd sent home an introductory letter, a digital survey, and made a few "good calls home" that I try to do to every students' family to start the year. However, I was not familiar with my students' families yet, except for those whose siblings I had taught. Thank God for those relationships though because little did I know, but I was soon to experience one of the most disturbing weekends of my life!

A parent took it upon themselves to post their belief that I was promoting Black Lives Matter because I drew a parallel to the protests in the 1960's as a part of the introductory material. In 2020, the book had clear parallels to our lives of protests, disrupted families, and the psychological element was intriguing. This created quite the discussion, but my intention was clear: make the novel relevant to teenagers by setting up comparisons that would activate their prior knowledge and relate to the current state of affairs in their world. I didn't love the drama surrounding this, but the part I want to share here, that I didn't share in the second edition of *The Flexible SEL Classroom*, is about another layer to the story, the layer that is actually more concerning than a parent with a different political opinion.

As if having my content challenged wasn't concerning enough, even though I could easily defend it, it became apparent that a more sinister situation was happening. Another parent of one of my students posted in the "community" forum a brand new post, one that ignored this first drama entirely and instead accused me of being "sick" and stating that they thought it was really disgusting that her child would be made to learn about serial killers. They went on to post pictures of my assignment (which made no sense as a part of this so-called "serial killer" unit I was doing). Until that weekend, I had no idea that where I live in western New York, there is a local legend about a different Pigman, a serial killer who supposedly killed three teenage boys. There's even a road called Pigman Road.

They then asked the forum to weigh in on what my motives might be. The hate that was spewed about how disgusting I was, how I had no morals, etc. was frightening. The assignment was critiqued, my role as union president was brought up, and even my success as an author was dragged through the mud. There was literally nothing I could do about what was being posted, even though it made no sense, wasn't true, and just stirred up a bunch of people who didn't know me at all. This entire thread was in the same forum, ostensibly with the same readers who had just been discussing what my political agenda was, and yet the conversation continued. I quickly learned that those who simply scroll for drama, don't read for details.

Finally, after dozens of people sent me screenshots, the parents of a former student defended me, stating that there was clearly a misunderstanding, that I was teaching *The Pigman,* a novel set in 1968 that had nothing to do with our local legend. They even pointed out the other thread that was posted and asked if anyone had actually asked me about any of this! They provided my school email, my Twitter, and my website.

NO ONE, not one person, reached out to me to find out what was going on. The weekend was miserable. By Sunday night, I was simply sick from fear, annoyance, and I was completely deflated. Is this what we'd come to? Finally, around 6:00 that Sunday, a parent of one of the students who was actually in my class posted a long message, reiterating that the assignment was about the book, a classic, and that the lesson made complete sense in context, and that their son was already interested and had just completed his first reading assignment. The response from the original poster was almost worse than the event: "LOL. I never liked English class." LOL. Hardly. My weekend had been miserable, my name had been bandied around all weekend in a negative context, and the accurate information had been readily available if anyone had wanted it. But they didn't. That's the point of those types of forums.

Now, luckily, I'm a National Board Certified, 2018 Association of Middle Level Educators Teacher of the Year, and president of a union, and an educator with 20 years of experience. I'm not saying this to brag, but I am saying this to be clear: this kind of attack is what drives younger, less experienced, less confident teachers to leave the profession. *It also shows the most dangerous aspect of social media, in my experience, and that is anyone can make accusations about you, even in the face of clear evidence otherwise, and most of the time, people who want to pile on can't wait to participate, and the voices of reason are easy to scroll right past.*

I'm almost 50 years old, and I'm comfortable with my own practice, reputation, and I am extremely transparent. However, I worry about my own daughter, a future teacher, who will be leaving for college by the time this book is published. If this were to happen to her, it is hard to know how she'd react. Moreover, it is hard to know how to prepare a person for such a public position as teaching, but in this chapter I'll try to prepare new teachers and their mentors with some "lessons learned." *Let's take a look at the Social Media Dilemma.*

- ◆ Facebook and The Parent (Friend) Trap
- ◆ Teacher Twitter/Instagram/ Tik Tok
- ◆ Student Privacy
- ◆ Public Servant

Facebook and the parent (friend) trap

There's nothing quite like when you click with your students' parents. You work hard to develop relationships, and the effort pays off when you see the "friend request." Who doesn't like friend requests, right? Wrong. Don't fall for the Parent (Friend) Trap. While being friendly with your students' parents is quite rewarding, you need to avoid the Facebook relationship until after you no longer teach their child. You can come up with your own canned phrase, but I always put a little blurb in my family letter that says,

> I am sure we will become great friends as we experience your child's 8th grade year with me! Feel free to send me a Facebook friend request, next year, when you can tell me all about their high school experience!

It saves me from awkward situations. With that being said, there are loads of reasons that you shouldn't be friends with parents of current students on Facebook, but I'll share three that are most straightforward.

The first reason is simply professionalism. I am not friends with my principal on Facebook (you shouldn't be either). I like my principal. I'd even attend social events with them, but I don't want the person who is my direct supervisor to be deeply woven into my life. I get it. The world is a giant social media network. But, it is important to keep some separation, and the fact is, your students' caregivers are your bosses. I don't mean this in, "I pay taxes, so I pay your salary" way that gets thrown around by some, but I do mean that teachers are constantly critiqued, and giving your students' caregivers ammunition isn't wise.

About a decade ago, when Facebook was less hateful, I chronicled a very topsy-turvy roadtrip with my husband, seven year old, four year old, and elderly mother-in-law. Frankly, there wasn't anything about the roadtrip that I retrospectively see as particularly chaotic, given the travelers who were with me, but I was younger and less experienced then. In any event, on Sunday, the day we were returning home before I had school on Monday, my husband got food poisoning about four hours from our house. We HAD to get a hotel and let my husband ride it out in the privacy of a hotel while I kept the kiddos occupied at the pool. I called myself out of work for that Monday since we had no chance of getting home for school the next day.

I had made the mistake of "checking-in" on Facebook at the hotel and posting pictures of my adorable kiddos at the pool. Of course, I didn't take pictures of my grayish-green husband, nor did I document his horrors, nor did I complain that we had to spend an extra 300 dollars that we didn't have to get hotel rooms for my mother-in-law and us. This is social media, right? You paint the picture without the glaring or garish parts.

On Monday, a parent noted on my Facebook that it sure looked like we were having fun instead of teaching students. This was not a parent of one of my students, but a parent I knew loosely whose child went to the middle school where I taught. Now, I wasn't about to get into all of this on Facebook to explain, but when I returned to school on Tuesday, my principal called me down to ask about the situation. Back then, I wasn't a union leader, and I was scared to death. The truth is, I had taken a family sick day, and I didn't need to explain a thing. That's what family sick days are for. However, it put me and my principal in an awkward position, and I regretted clicking "accept" of a friend request from an acquaintance. I explained to my principal, in probably more detail than he'd hoped for, and things were fine. I had, inadvertently, opened myself up to more scrutiny, and the lesson stung.

What should you take away from these anecdotes? First, this isn't simply a Facebook issue, of course, but I do find that there's a certain brand of drama found in the forums that are hosted there that I don't find elsewhere. I'm not suggesting that you don't have a Facebook, or that you don't chronicle your life—I do—but I am warning that you have to be extremely careful of the perceptions that others will have, even if they aren't accurate. Avoid the biggest drama by not accepting friend requests from students' caregivers.

Teacher Twitter/Instagram/Tik Tok

I teach a few college classes for future teachers, and one of the things I always make students do is create a "Teacher Twitter," Instagram, or Tik Tok. They are instructed to use a professional name that doesn't include numbers, underlining, or anything that could be misconstrued. My Twitter handle is @MsAmberChandler, and it is easy to find, by design. In my district, I regularly sit on hiring committees, and I always Google candidates. There are three outcomes from my Google search.

First, if you don't have any social media presence, then I find nothing, which isn't very interesting, or I find your 10th grade lacrosse photo that ran in a local paper. Cute, but it won't help you land a job. Though we are facing a teaching shortage right now, that won't always be the case, and if you are up against someone who has more "out there in the world," you could lose out. In some districts, particularly those whose students have one-to-one devices, utilize social media for their communication, and think of themselves as 21st century connected, a person with no presence might seem like they don't know how to engage versus those who chose not to.

On the other hand, there are those whose social media presence game is on point—if they are not trying to be a teacher. Photos of wine-tasting weekends, their new Sperry boots, engagement rings, and pumpkin spice lattes. I'm not knocking these social media mavens and misters, but I am warning that if that is all you have out in the world, I might go down the rabbit hole and see which Kate Spade collection you recommend, but I won't be wowed. Don't get me wrong, this is a completely acceptable social media presence, but there's a third category of social media presence that can boost your marketability.

The final category is those who have an educational presence. These teachers and teachers-to-be are reading quality feeds like *EdWeek*, *Edutopia*, *WeAreTeachers*, *ShareMyLesson*, and content-specific spaces like @artwithjennyk, @keslerscience, @mathgiraffe, *Middleweb,* and *AMLE* (Association of Middle Level Educators). They are sharing links, writing blogs, and generally participating in their profession using social media. My daughter is a Pinterest enthusiast, and she follows all kinds of interesting educators on Tik Tok as well. As a high schooler, she isn't creating much content (though she did have a guest blog on *Middleweb* when she was in the 8th grade that has 29 comments!). However, I'll be helping her create a website where she can document her educational journey as a college student and build a digital portfolio.

As for your own personal social media, simply realize that hiring committees, parents, and especially your students will look for you online. *Almost all of us have a digital footprint, and if you can keep in mind that teaching is an exceptionally public adventure, you'll be fine.* Your privacy settings should be set to their narrowest audience. There are some people who will go out of their way to use the simplest things against teachers (remember the Pigman story?), so being aware is your best bet. Some people ask me if they can post the wine trail picture. Yes, if you are of age. Yes, you can post a tasteful picture, but I'd take it at stop number one, not mid-afternoon day drinking. I try to think about my harshest critic, consider what they'd say about what I post, and use that to help me calibrate.

Despite all of these warnings, I'm extremely active on Twitter particularly. I only follow educators or education related people, so it weeds out a lot of junk. My Twitterverse is filled with amazing educators, challenging conversations, and a ridiculous number of free resources. There's a bunch of inspirational content, and I always enjoy the relationships I develop through Twitter chats and my professional associations. I give my college students a list of "must follows" in education. Here's my current ten educators to follow, in no particular order: @beyondthedesk, @Pfagell, @blocht574, @alfiekohn,

Student privacy

Of all the conversations we can have about social media, this one has the most clear-cut answer: *Do not post pictures of students without the consent of their caregiver, in writing.* Schools have a "Do Not Photograph" list of students, but that isn't enough. If you plan to post a picture, you have to have permission from the caregiver, no matter if they aren't on the "Do Not Photograph" list. I am a stickler for this one for a few reasons.

First, there are the legal and safety consequences. You do not know the particular students' complex custodial issues or the reasons that their families may not want them on social media. The form to opt a student out of photos is often distributed at the beginning of the year, in the midst of dozens of papers. It would be easy for a caregiver to miss the form, and by failing to fill it out give the district the impression that it is ok to photograph their child and share publicly. That's fine for the district to take the "opt out only" approach, but as a new teacher—or even a veteran one—I highly recommend that you get permission.

Second, there is respect for the children themselves. I haven't posted an image publicly of my son without his consent in a few years. He's a freshman, and that consent barely ever happens. When he was little, and didn't care, my posts were indulgent and he was fine with the cuteness deluge. Out of respect for him, I beg for a picture for holidays or major events, and I still don't always get them. Our students are entitled to their privacy as well, and in this day and age, if your teacher posts a picture on Twitter, it can easily be manipulated into a disparaging meme. I let my students know when I'm going to take a picture, when I'm going to post it, and promise them that I will never post them eating or in an unflattering photo. I usually Tweet a picture at the end of a class, so I ask, on the spot, can I use the photo and show them the tweet for context. To this end, I've had students who will let me one day and not the next—and that is their prerogative.

We are role models of how our students should act as digital citizens. Do I want them to take pictures of me? Posting to their social media accounts about me? Quoting what I say or putting my assignments on social media? These are tough questions to ask ourselves, but I do think we should consider this. I had a student who was always taking pictures in my room. I honestly didn't have an issue with it per se, but I was worried what she was using them for. I was pleased that she was positive about it, telling me that she was sharing our flexible seating with her friend at another school. However, that twinge of fear reminded me that it is a truly vulnerable position that we are putting students in when we use their images and work on social media.

Finally, and this should go without saying, but never, ever, ever follow your students, interact with them on social media platforms, or comment on their posts. Even if your intentions are pristine, there is zero way to protect an adult who is communicating with a student outside school hours on platforms that are designed to socialize. Additionally, these platforms have age requirements (Snapchat, Facebook, and Tik Tok are 13, Instagram is 16, and all of the social media platforms have language around parental permission, though it isn't verified in any way) which many students don't follow. You don't want to be involved in any way with social media and minors.

Public servant

Finally, I'm going to say something that might be an "unpopular opinion." As educators, we should never complain about our jobs, our pay, our families, or our students in posts on social media (I use the word post here purposefully. Keep reading.) We shouldn't complain about late buses, lack of choices in the cafeteria, or the poor quality of student work. We shouldn't complain, in posts, period.

By posts, I mean the one off tweets, Facebook post, or other social media that is done in a hurry. Complaining is an art for some people, and I think it is crucial that we vent somewhere, but it makes our jobs incredibly difficult when there are constant choruses of complaints that are largely unexplained or unsubstantiated. Also off limits is any type of countdown until we get a break, any keyboard raging about disinterested parents, "discipline starts in the home," and how you'd raise your children to be different than those kiddos in your classroom.

We are public servants. Our job is one of the most crucial in society, and we diminish it, and create an unprofessional environment sometimes because our "clients" don't directly pay us. Think of it this way. Have you ever been scrolling and come across a doctor doubting their patient's pain? A lawyer mocking their clients' lack of judgment? An accountant belittling the savings plan of their customers? See what I mean? We want to be treated as professionals, yet we are sometimes our worst enemies. Don't believe me? Let me give you some examples in a very short study in social media while I took a coffee break.

Here's what I found: a "countdown to Christmas" (mind you, it is also before Thanksgiving as I write this, so it makes the teacher seem like they are dying to escape their job), a teacher who posted how many assignments she had to grade and warned students not to ask her how they did on it (wouldn't interest in their work be a good thing?), and the worst one are the "Things Teachers Say In Their Heads" that lists things like "sit your ass down" and "shut the f*$% up." The last example is from a group made up of educators who post memes about our job. Remember the forum I was attacked in? It seems a lot like that one.

This all brings me to the Social (Media) Dilemma, which is a bit of wordplay around the very important movie, *The Social Dilemma*, which is included in my book *Movie Magic*. The fact is, there is a very real need for educators to be a part of the social media world because it is a reflection of society and where many people get their news and information. We must be a presence, fully knowing we might be unjustly attacked. We must be a presence, knowing that we are judged harshly, but we must work to change the narrative about teaching and social media is one of the best venues to do so.

As I mentioned, I used the word "post" purposefully. I highly recommend that you write blogs, opinion pieces, researched white papers, submit to online education platforms, and write for peer reviewed journals. All of that will be shared on social media, but the difference is that your thoughts are well-developed, you have a chance to create clarity around topics instead of muddy them, and frankly, it is simply delayed action. In the moment, I've wanted to fire off a post about state testing, but by writing an opinion piece, I have time to craft what I want to say, measure how it will be received, and consider the risk/reward trade-off.

This isn't an easy topic, and I am certain that I've missed some nuances that are generational. However, I do know that I've watched social media almost destroy careers, and I've personally benefited from my own social media savvy. As you begin your career, use the following "Mentoring Moment" to talk with another teacher, a parent, friends, or your mentor about these important topics.

Mentoring moment

After reading this chapter, use these questions to help you be intentional about your decisions and actions. Remember to ask questions, take some notes, and explore the topic with a trusted friend, parent, role model, or mentor.

1. Have you ever felt harmed by social media? How did the situation happen? If not, how have you protected yourself from the negative aspects of social media?
2. Do you have a professional social media presence? If so, consider how to boost your interactions. If not, think about ways to participate in your profession online.
3. Is there anything in your personal social media that might need "cleaning up?" Are there any posts that you'd be better off taking down? How might you handle this topic in the future?

Resources

Davis, Caroline. "Public School Teachers and Social Media: The Protections and Limitations of the Right to Free Speech." Boston Lawyer Blog, Zalkind, Duncan, and Berntein, 6 Sept. 2022, https://www.bostonlawyerblog.com/public-school-teachers-and-social-media-the-protections-and-limitations-of-the-right-to-free-speech/.

Mattson, Brynne, et al. "How to Build a Social Media Presence as a Teacher." *Ace.edu*, American College of Education, 29 Apr. 2019, https://www.ace.edu/blog/post/2019/04/25/how-to-build-a-social-media-presence-as-a-teacher.

3

You don't know what you don't know

Institutional knowledge

Imagine, for a minute, that you must walk into a random house for Thanksgiving Dinner. Your goal: convince the family there to invite you back for the next year. First, you might bring a bottle of wine, right? Well, maybe. Or, if it is like my childhood home, there is no alcohol allowed. Next, you think of small talk topics

- ♦ Logistics
- ♦ Key players
- ♦ Key ideas
- ♦ Past failures
- ♦ Building lore
- ♦ No fail tips

that might be good. I'm from Buffalo, so the Bills are always a great bet. However, at this particular dinner there's an ex Bill's fan who will want to tell a very long story about the year he

DOI: 10.4324/9781003365921-3

lost his faith in the hometown team, leading to a real downer of a dinner. Maybe you decide to bring a pecan pie. Who doesn't love a pecan pie? How were you to know that Aunt Millie has brought the secret-ingredient pecan pie for the last 25 years? The secret ingredient is love, and now some stranger has tried to one-up her. If this sounds like an impossible task, I'll let you in on this secret: joining a new school is like joining a family. The good news is, I'm going to share some tips with you that will hopefully help you get invited back the next year!

Logistics

One of the most nerve-wracking things about being new is the seemingly endless logistics involved in getting from the parking lot to your classroom, and then making it through the day. Every school has unwritten rules that no one thinks to share with you. For example, if parking isn't assigned, then you can bet that the teachers who have been there for two decades, nearly before you were even born, have a favorite spot. Don't think that the amazing spot by the door is yours. It is not. If it seems too good to be true, it is. It is probably Mr F's spot and has been for as long as anyone can remember. Save yourself the weird animosity by parking in empty spots that are not directly by the building or in the first rows. I know this is petty, and that is why I call it weird animosity. However, teachers are, more than anything, creatures of habit. As a newbie, I'd avoid tangling with anyone, even if it seems (and is) silly.

There are a few logistics you'll need to figure out a few important logistics very soon. Where is the staff bathroom? Faculty room? Mailboxes? Then, you'll need to drill down a little more to find out if it is ever acceptable to go to the students' bathrooms because sometimes you gotta go! You'll need to find out who eats in the faculty room and if not there, where are you supposed to go? How often should you check your mailbox? You'll need to understand the emergency plans for a fire drill, hold in place, and lockdown. None of this is covered in orientation, right? (I'm sure there are exceptions!) Many districts assume that this information is gleaned from mentors or teachers you will work with, but there is nothing that can rattle your confidence more than hearing a fire alarm and realizing that you have no idea what you are supposed to do or where you are supposed to go. (If you are desperate, follow the teacher closest to your room)

I'm not trying to scare you, but the fact is, as a new teacher, you don't know what you don't know. It is my hope that mentors are using this book with you and will be able to give you the answers to these logistical questions. Don't blame anyone for not thinking of the logistics, but it will help if you nail down the answers to the questions above, as well as a few others that are completely *not* academic. Make sure to go through the questions at the end of the chapter with a mentor or someone who works at the school with you!

I'm a mentor, and last year my poor mentee was ridiculously sick. She started to drive to work, but couldn't even make it. She texted me in a panic. She knew how to use the computer system to put in for an absence, but who did she call in this situation? I know your first thought is that you can **not** be sick your first year. In a post-Covid age, you are encouraged to stay home if you are ill. However, if you push through, you need to respect the fact that there are some illnesses that you can't talk yourself through with some Advil, a Coke, and a Reese's cup (Trust me, if you have a horrible headache, this is a go-to. Don't judge.) To be blunt, if you are vomiting or have a stomach bug of any sort, don't come to school. Ever. All of this is to say that there are logistical questions that you don't want to learn as you go. Make sure to use the questions at the end of the chapter to help you prepare.

Key players

When I was hired, there were three Marcia's who were constantly referred to. One Marcia was the secretary, and I learned pretty quickly that the secretary is always the most important person in the building. Another Marcia was definitely a key player, as she had been teaching at the middle school for decades and knew everyone. She'd taught entire generations of families. The last Marcia was from our central office, and though she wasn't in touch often, when she was, you had to pay attention. In my first days, my head was spinning trying to figure out which Marcia was being referenced. If my rosters over the years indicate any-thing, the workplace is going to be overloaded with Maddie, Madison, and Madelyns right about now and give it five years and there will be Isabella, Bella, Izzys, Bell, and Annabelles. Make sure you learn who the key players are, and make sure to send your email to the correct one!

I've recommended for years that districts create a yearbook type document for new teachers, and I'm always excited when people change their avatars to their headshots. (Always do this! You want people to connect your name with your emails. Absolutely do not make your icon a dog, an apple, or anything else that is what my dad would call "cutesy." You want to be pro-fessional. Your doctor does not use a stethoscope as her avatar). Remember that you are likely one of many new hires, and as you are introduced, try to connect and reiterate your name and make sure you are learning theirs!

Once you sort out names, you then need to sit back and pay attention to whom everyone turns for answers. This is often a department chair or team leader, but just as often it is simply a veteran teacher who has "seen some things." *I know lots of people warn against becoming friendly with the grizzled old vet-erans, but I disagree. Don't let their demeanor rub off on you, but they are often the same people who have the ear of administra-tion and most of the time their bark is worse than their bite.*

When I first started teaching at Portsmouth High School, I was, to say the least, a bit eager. I knew what I wanted. I wanted to be the AP teacher who inspired and taught her students so well that they received the highest scores, and I the highest pass rates. I wanted to become a department chair when my beloved mentor, Mary Potter, retired. I knew that I wanted to teach college classes. This is quite a vision for a new teacher who didn't know how to do much of anything when it came to the day-to-day operations of the job. One day I walked into the lunch room, which was three long tables end to end. About 20 people would eat there each day. I had been warned not to hang out in the teachers' lounges, so I'd been eating in my room. This was a huge missed opportunity, but some veterans got me sorted out quick.

Anyway, I checked my mailbox, and there was a memo (this was going on 25 years ago) that I wanted to talk to Mary, my mentor about. I walked over to her seat at the table and basically interrupted the friendly banter, assuming that Mary would love to talk about it with me over her tuna salad sandwich. That is when a teacher we'll call Hal yelled from his end of the table, "Hey blondie. We don't talk shop at lunch. Pull up a chair but you can't talk school." Set aside that he called me blondie—which was both not that unusual even in the late 90's and also verification that he didn't know who I was. He'd embarrassed me, but he'd also invited me into the circle, which was more like a giant oblong. I turned on my heel, tears welling up, and left.

I avoided the lunchroom for awhile, but somehow Hal, who was in my department, didn't let up. He was always around, always subtly or not so subtly pointing out my "newbie" status. Finally, one day I was checking my mail, and he was complaining about the fact that we were getting computers in our rooms. His assertion (and wow did he turn out to be right!) was that this "time saver" was going to take up all of our time. Now I know that he was insanely prophetic, but at the time, I'd had enough. I whirled around, and without thinking said, "Hal, that is because you are a dinosaur. You've been teaching longer than I've been alive, and I'm tired of you making me feel that I'm stupid just because I'm young." He whistled through his teeth, said, "Atta girl. Now you've arrived," and walked away. He never singled me out after that, and I eventually did eat lunch at the table, and looking back, taking time to not talk shop over a meal with your faculty family is an excellent idea.

I tell this story to demonstrate a few points. First, be considerate of the norms of your school. If I'd paid any attention to anyone except myself, I would have noticed that no one else was talking shop at lunch. If I'd paid attention, I'd know that Hal was the resident jokester and was razzing me just like he did everyone else. Instead, my fear was juxtaposed with ambition, and I was putting off a weird vibe to everyone. It seemed like I was an unfriendly know-it-all, while I was really an insecure new teacher who LOVED teaching and couldn't imagine why anyone would complain. Then again, I hadn't been doing it for two decades, and I hadn't experienced the ups and downs of this family. I was a person who'd showed up to Thanksgiving dinner and didn't try to assimilate myself; instead, I'd been busy asserting myself. Now luckily, this particular family was very forgiving and allowed me to come back the next year, but I did so with my eyes wide open to observe. A few years later when I moved to New York, this faculty family had a huge going away party for that newbie who'd dared to talk shop, and I'll never forget the first school family who helped me to understand what institutional history was.

When I moved to my new district, I understood that I needed to look out for the key players. They aren't always who you might expect. It could be Marcia the secretary or Hal the resident wisecracker. It could be a guidance counselor and it could be the teacher all the students always come back to visit. As we all know, all families are different, and it takes awhile to learn how we fit into the dynamic. Rest assured, you will find your place, but it will not be overnight.

The people in your building have been "doing life" together for many years, as teaching is still a one and done career in a world where people job hop regularly. Teachers generally stay put. We consider it a big move to change grade levels or buildings. The family you walk into has been together through bad bosses, deaths in families, births, maternity leaves, and now, a pandemic. If you are lucky, you will land in a tight knit school. It may take a bit of time, but you will be able to weave yourself into the fabric of their family.

In addition to the teachers in your building, you need to be aware of all administrators in the district who might ever be in your building. Usually this will entail your principal, assistant principals, a curriculum director or coordinator, the assistant superintendent, and the superintendent. There are others, but if you know these, you'll be ok. Again, not to scare you, but any of these people can stroll into your classroom at any time, and it will go much more smoothly if you are able to stop your lesson and say, "Welcome Mrs. D."

Key ideas

Another really important part of institutional history is the key ideas that are central to the school. These aren't always the most profound, but many times they are widely held. I think of it like this—are you a Coke family, Pepsi family, or a "we don't drink soda" family? In all three scenarios, people are pretty committed and opinionated about their choice. Schools can often be like this, and it isn't always a bad thing. For example, when I moved from my high school family in New Hampshire to a middle school in New York, I learned pretty quickly that almost every decision was made around the idea of teaming. Schedules, staffing, and pretty much everything else was centered on this middle school mainstay. Having come from a high school, I wasn't used to the emphasis on teaming, as my prior school had been mainly divided into departments, as most high schools are. Teaming makes a ton of sense for middle schools, and I soon learned to think about a students' experience in terms of their whole school day vs how they performed in English.

Another area where schools' philosophies or key ideas differ widely is their approach to special education. The law allows a wide array of programming meant to service students who have academic or emotional struggles. This can include inclusion classes, self-contained classes, behavior classrooms, consultant teachers, and many others. At some schools, inclusion classrooms are co-taught by a special education teacher and regular education teacher where the responsibility is equally divided while other schools' inclusion model calls for a lead teacher and a special education teacher acting more as a support. For as many models of special education, there are also variables in each scenario.

If you are a regular education teacher who is assigned to work with a special education teacher, please take the time to find out "how things are done." We could debate what should be done, but when you are new you have to learn to work within the parameters that are already mapped out. Why? So that you will eventually get the respect, seniority, and voice that can impact policy and procedures! We need new voices and ideas, and we really could use some solutions for our special education students, but when veteran teachers understand the red tape and problems and a newbie comes in and tell them how they aren't doing a good job, it sets up a horrible work environment where those who lose the most are students. This is true for all of the systems that you'll encounter in schools—they aren't perfect, but change is incremental, often at a snails' pace, because just one change has an exponential impact.

Past failures

One reason that schools are often reticent to new ideas and change is that almost every institution has had a failure of some sort that became the defining story in some poor administrator's life. I remember in my early years, I said something like, "I don't know. Maybe this isn't the worst idea," and a veteran teacher responded, "You're right. But we tried it in 1985, and they used it to cut teaching positions." If I had the time and were somehow able to take a break from teaching, I'd immediately pursue a doctorate to study the impact of institutional knowledge on the success of a district. I assert that the districts where institutional knowledge is systematically shared and equally disseminated to administrators and teachers, there is better cooperation and the results for students are improved. However, this is often not the case, so if someone meets your idea with what seems like excessive resistance, ask around to find out what history you can learn that might help you to find another approach.

Building lore

My favorite story of all the stories—and I don't know any of the "characters" since it is building lore—is about a teacher who was retiring. Apparently, she had taught when smoking was allowed at school, as crazy as that sounds, and she'd been irritated when it had been banned. The local lore was that on her last day of school she had roller skated out of the building smoking a cigarette and waving at everyone. I'll be honest. I don't even care if this story is true or not, as it has made me smile every time I think of it for decades! *These stories abound in every district, and are just like family lore. Some may be exaggerated, but no matter what, these stories should be encouraged and respected, as we all know that stories weave our individual lives together.*

In Hamburg, right outside of Buffalo, where I teach now, we have a lot of snow. Currently, I'm writing this since I'm snowed in with around 70 inches of snow—around 5 feet 10 inches—of snow. We've had the October storm, then we had Snowvember, and they are calling this Snowvember 2.0 since it is happening the same week as the original. One of the stories of district lore is when teachers and an administrator got snowed into school with students. I'm sure it wasn't a picnic at the time, but everyone loves to joke that we'll be snowed in, just like it happened before.

When you hear these stories, consider it a gift. You are being invited in to the building lore, and by listening you are implicitly becoming a part of the family. Ask questions. Beg for more details. Make the story a part of your collective knowledge of the school and the district. So, when someone seems to give a certain administrator more slack, it might just be because she made PBJs and watched movies with small children, stranded away from their families, making sure to let each of them call their families. She might have made it into a party that became the stuff of stories, and if things don't always look or seem "fair," remember that there are always a lot of stories that shape the collective institutional narrative at the center of a building's lore.

No fail tips

With so much to consider, how might one ever ingratiate themselves into a new building and district? There are some "no fail tips" that I've gathered from those who came before me whose institutional knowledge was handed down to me. Here they are:

◆ Listen more. Talk less. You will have plenty of time to contribute.
◆ Ask for help when you need it. It is a compliment to be asked for help.
◆ Allow others to help you. Serving and supporting newer teachers is invigorating for veterans.
◆ Never "talk crap" about another teacher to students or families. You don't have to agree with everyone, but you do need to present a united front.
◆ Rumors fly in schools. Stay out of gossip.
◆ Say thank you often. Putting it in writing is even nicer. Everyone loves a heartfelt card.
◆ Try to defer to your "elders" when you can. Your time will come.
◆ Don't be afraid to volunteer, but don't do more than you can handle. It's better to be great at two things than mediocre at five.
◆ Manners and humility go a long way.

If my advice for this chapter sounds like an "oldie" talking to you, it's because I am older, and I mentor new teachers every year unofficially, and I have been the official/district assigned mentor to eight teachers. The new teachers who are able to ingratiate themselves with the "family" do much better than those who don't. I'm not saying that you won't ever be able to express your every thought and opinion (though that isn't a good idea for anyone!), but I am saying that if you treat your first few years like a Thanksgiving guest—happy to be there, polite, friendly, willing to help out—your chances of being invited back are much better!

Mentoring moment

Use the following checklist to ready yourself for the new "family" you are about to join. Once you've filled out the questions, find someone in your new "family" who can help you determine if your answers are correct or if you need some guidance.

◆ The best place for me to **park** is _____.

◆ If I'm sick, and I can't get to my computer, call _____.

◆ I know the safety directions and how to handle a fire drill, hold in place, and a lockdown. The safety folder is located _____.

◆ The nearest bathroom is _____ _____.

◆ If something happens in my classroom, and I need help, call extension _____.

◆ To dial out, and reach 911, I need to dial _____.

◆ My head building representative (or trusted veteran teacher if you don't have a union) is _____ extension _____.

◆ To get copies, I use the code _____ or send them to _____. The copiers are located _____.

◆ I have an emergency bag at school with:
  • A fresh set of clothes and undergarments
  • Deodorant

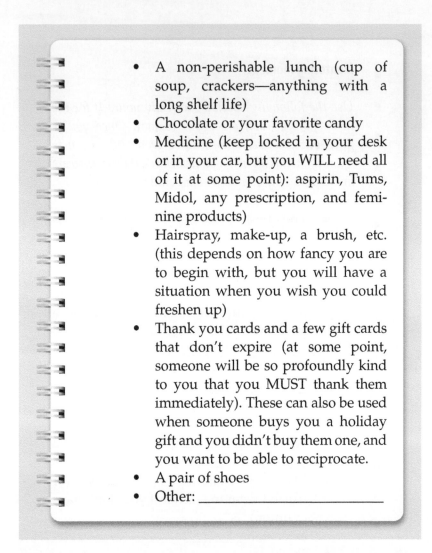

- A non-perishable lunch (cup of soup, crackers—anything with a long shelf life)
- Chocolate or your favorite candy
- Medicine (keep locked in your desk or in your car, but you WILL need all of it at some point): aspirin, Tums, Midol, any prescription, and feminine products)
- Hairspray, make-up, a brush, etc. (this depends on how fancy you are to begin with, but you will have a situation when you wish you could freshen up)
- Thank you cards and a few gift cards that don't expire (at some point, someone will be so profoundly kind to you that you MUST thank them immediately). These can also be used when someone buys you a holiday gift and you didn't buy them one, and you want to be able to reciprocate.
- A pair of shoes
- Other: _____

Resources

"15 Must Read Tips for Success as a First Year Teacher." *Differentiated Teaching*, 18 Feb. 2022, https://www.differentiatedteaching.com/tips-for-first-year-teachers/.

Education, Novak. "Advice for New Teachers in Their First Year of Teaching." *Novak Education, Novak Educational Consulting*, 1 Aug. 2022, https://www.novakeducation.com/blog/advice-for-new-teachers-in-their-first-year-of-teaching.

Ketcham, Sarah. "A Very Practical Guide for First-Year Teachers." *Share My Lesson, American Federation of Teachers*, 2 Sept. 2015, https://sharemylesson.com/blog/very-practical-guide-first-year-teachers.

Staff, WeAreTeachers. "20 Things New Teachers Really, Really Need to Know (According to the Vets)." *We Are Teachers*, 18 July 2017, https://www.weareteachers.com/20-things-new-teachers-really-really-need-to-know-according-to-the-vets-2/.

4

A meeting for you ... and another meeting for you!

When trying to explain the definition of the word "jargon" to my 8th grade students, my co-teacher Laura and I have a little fun. As we start class, this is the conversation that we'll begin with:

AMBER: *"Don't forget the faculty meeting today."*
LAURA: *"Where is it? Are we supposed to sit with our PLCs?"*
AMBER: *"No, I think you take your SLO data and sit with your department."*
LAURA: *"I hope we aren't doing gap analysis. I'd rather talk about plans for SEL integration in advisory."*

This would also make a good intro to acronyms, but we ask students, "What are we talking about?" Most understand that we are going to a school meeting, but that's about it. We explain that jargon is specialized language that is used by a particular group—in our case, teachers. Truth be told, if you are a new teacher, the above conversation would probably make your head spin too! That's ok. Every new situation involves new vocabulary, and it is very difficult to grasp in those first months as so much is coming at you. In this chapter, I'm going to share some insights about a long list of meetings you'll be invited to, "volun-told" to attend, or required to participate in as a committee member. Wait? You didn't know you were on a committee? You will be, don't worry!

DOI: 10.4324/9781003365921-4

- Faculty meetings
- Department meetings
- Grade-level meetings
- Team meetings
- Data meetings
- IEP and 504 meetings
- Pre-conferences
- Post-conferences
- Disciplinary
- Tenure

Faculty meetings

There's a whole bunch of memes about faculty meetings. They are, for the most part, accurate. A faculty meeting is a great place to learn about your fellow teachers, and rest assured it is a great place for people to learn about you as well. I'll try to break it to you gently, but there's no good way to say this: if it's only "been a minute" since you have been hired, do not talk. Don't ask a question. There is a better, smaller venue to ask questions. A principal I had years ago used to say, "Are there any questions that are for the good of the order?" What he meant by this was, "Don't waste all of our time with a question that is only rele-vant to you or a few others." This, to me, is actually the height of leadership; he understood that our time was valuable, and he respected that.

Having a full audience isn't the time to share either. Really, no matter how relevant it is, don't try to tell a staff who have been teaching longer than you've been alive about this great example you have from your student teaching placement. Faculty meetings are novel for new teachers, but most of us have sat through hundreds, and even amongst the veteran staff, we have an issue with teachers who like to hear themselves talk.

I know I'm sounding brutal here, but I'm wearing my "teacher mom" hat, and I promise you that I will say all of this to my daughter before her first faculty meeting. Why would I warn her? The same reason I'm warning you: you don't want an entire audience of people judging you for your exuberance when all that is between them and the end of their day is a story about student teaching.

Don't think that we are disgruntled and disinterested in engaging in academic discourse—we aren't. But, for the most part, a faculty meeting could have been an email. Sure, there are exceptions, but it is important to understand that in education the real conversations, the real learning and collaborating happen in small groups, amongst those who are really interested versus the faculty version of "forced family fun." Most veteran teachers look at faculty meetings as a chance to catch up before and after with teachers who are across the building from us or we don't see often. So, my pro-tip for you in regards to faculty meetings is this: find a friendly face, enjoy some great small talk, and enjoy the people watching.

Department meetings

When my kiddos were younger, we taught them that at any time they (or us) could call a family meeting. At the family meeting, they could bring up any changes that needed to be made, "put something on our schedule," or make a request. As a family, we know each other really well, and there's been plenty of interrupting, finishing each others' sentences, and reminders of past successes and failures. For example, in my house, and maybe yours, there is a serious sock issue. No one ever has socks. We buy them at an alarming rate, and yet there is never enough. We gave up on matching socks well before my kiddos ever went to school, and we make no pretenses about our disorganization in this area.

Over the years, we've tried many strategies proposed by well-meaning moms who have a longer attention span for such things than I do. We've tried bins, socks of all the same color, and everyone being responsible for their own socks. In any event, when I bring this topic up, it is often met with groans, "Remember, that didn't work," and the like, as well as reminders of some things that worked for awhile and no one can remember why we don't do it that way anymore. In this way, my family meeting is akin to a department meeting: you share a history, often have to rehash things that have happened over many years, and everyone feels a bit possessive over their ideas, and somewhat critical of everyone else. No matter what though, there is a sense that you are all "in this together" whether you are talking about new ideas or rehashing successes and failures (the more epic the better).

I love the idea that people are in your life for a reason, a season, or a lifetime. *When thinking about your department, realize that administrators change, but for the most part, you'll spend many years "doing life" with all of its ups and downs with those in your department, so try to realize that these people are there for a lifetime.* To a new teacher, this can sound daunting, and perhaps a bit claustrophobic, but it is important to remember at the beginning that these are the people who will attend your retirement party.

Grade-level meetings

Grade-level meetings are similar to department meetings, but happen more at the elementary and middle levels. Most teachers end up teaching different grade levels over the years—sometimes by choice, but often because of fluxes in numbers, or in schools without unions, at the whim of an administrator. I'd view these meetings in the "season" category.

These meetings though are really important because they are to discuss curriculum, standards, and get to the meat of teaching and learning. I'd liken grade levels to teams. There is often someone who acts as the team captain, either as appointed by the district or just because they have been around and understand the ins and outs of things. Grade levels are frequently meeting to crunch data, measure growth, and compare the strategies that produce the greatest amount of growth. In these post-pandemic times, you'll probably hear a lot about gap closing and ways to accelerate learning.

One of my favorite quotes, "Comparison is the thief of joy," has been attributed to Theodore Roosevelt, C. S. Lewis, and Mark Twain, though none of them said it exactly, but it stands to reason that all of these thinkers understood that there is great pain in comparison, and I couldn't agree more. When you see another teacher's lesson plans or data binder or samples of student work, don't let the joy you had for *your* lesson plans, *your* data binder, or *your* darling student work be diminished. No classroom is the same, and the students in that classroom greatly impact how and what you are teaching.

That isn't to say that you don't learn from your colleagues and collaborate. One of the quickest ways to make teaching less of a 24-hour job is to learn to share the load with those teachers who are ostensibly in the same boat as you. Grade levels often meet to create lesson plans, and the load can be lessened when working together, but inequities will present themselves.

I'm not a very emotional person, but I cried angry tears at a grade-level meeting a few years ago, much to the shock of the other teachers. I am the President of our teachers union, go toe-to-toe with district administrators, and I have a reputation for being a bit of a stoic, so tears from me are unexpected. We were trying to pick a passage for our final exam reading comprehension section, and a teacher suggested a section of *Black Boy* by Richard Wright. I did not need to see the passage to know that a quarter of my students would not be able to access anything from the book. Yes, the Lexile Level is 950, and yes, the ATOS Reading Level is 7.4, so of course this is an appropriate suggestion for *that* teacher to make. The teacher did not have Special Education students, while I had 28 identified students, most reading at least two grade levels lower than their peers. In our discussion, the teacher rightfully made the argument that we can't make the test to meet the level of students we have, but rather according to the standards for 8th grade students. I agreed, but I was so angry.

I was angry because my students had made tremendous progress, learning so many important skills. They could put a link into a document, use a citation builder online, and write (mostly) complete sentences. They knew how to use resources when they didn't understand. Yet, here I was, creating an exam that they would surely not do very well on. I won't claim to have the answer here, and I could probably write a whole other book on how we should be assessing students, but I will say that schools are standardized, and grade levels need to work together to best meet the needs of *all* students. In the end though, what you do in your own classroom is your responsibility, and if you need to differentiate more than someone else, so be it.

Team meetings

Teaming is a middle school concept. The idea is that a team of core teachers will share the same students. The team of teachers will then be able to support the child across subject areas, and teams can create consistent expectations for homework, discipline, and parent communication. One of the best parts of teaming is that you learn more about your students. For example, I might learn that Suzy, who is really struggling in ELA, is actually a math and science whiz. Or, Billy might have told the team science teacher that he's having problems seeing the board, and the whole team can adjust.

When teams meet, they often come with data requested by a counselor or principal who is leading the meeting. How many students are failing? Are there any students who seem bored and could use some acceleration? Do we have any students with an attendance problem? Are there any behavioral trends we are noticing? These meetings are generally focused on a few students at a time, and the team often makes plans to intervene before a situation grows worse.

Teaming can also be great because one email from a group stating that Suzy needs to stay after school to make up a ton of missed assignments is better than five emails which will simply overwhelm the parent as much as the child. The downside of teaming is that you may be expected to conform to some common rule that you don't agree to. For example, I am the only person on my team who allows students unlimited retakes of tests, and I only put the highest score in my gradebook. This is pretty radical, and I don't try to push this onto my teammates. Rather, we work to support each other when we can, and allow our individual styles in our own classrooms.

Data meetings

I'm not a numbers person. I don't like talking about percentages, median scores, or the like. Many schools create data teams to talk about these numbers, and I have never once volunteered to be a part of that team. You will most likely not be required to be a part of those deeper and broader conversations that analyze trends, and drill down to "power standards" that a group may be struggling with. Always heed the data shared with you, as numbers do tell a story. I simply prefer my story to be told differently, but I never disregard what the hard facts tell me.

Even if you aren't a numbers person, every teacher will need to know how to access and think about their own classroom data, but thankfully much of this can be done through the LMS (Learning Management System) that your district uses. If you need help pulling that data from the LMS, seek out someone from the data team, a fellow department member, or a team member to help you. If they don't know how, they will know who you should ask.

I do a webinar about measuring the "real data." I'm not dismissive of the hard data, but as an SEL proponent, I think some other "data" should be studied way more closely by teachers. Here's a list of data topics that you might want to consider for your classroom, and once you are established (not a newbie), you might want to bring to the table:

   ◆ Which students appear not to have friends?
   ◆ Which students never speak throughout an entire day?
   ◆ Which students go to the nurse too much?

- ◆ Which students wear long sleeves or pants, even when it is hot? (Often to hide self-harm)
- ◆ Which students avoid going to lunch?
- ◆ Which students have had trauma? Divorce? Death? Downgrade in finances?

The list could go on and on, but you get the point. These pieces of data don't show up in presentations for the public and the Board of Education, but if you want to address deficits in your classroom, or close gaps, this is the data you should mine for ways to help your students.

IEP and 504 meetings

Individual Education Plans (IEPs) and 504's (named after Section 504 of the Rehabilitation Act of 1973, a civil rights law that prohibits discrimination against individuals with disabilities) are very important for our students who need additional supports to be successful in school. IEPs require specialized instruction to be offered, while 504s call for modifications and accommodations to be made, but not necessarily a difference in programming. They are both legal documents which must be followed. They are not suggestions, but instead directives. If I sound stern about this, it is because this is one area where teachers can find themselves in trouble.

Before I talk about the meetings, I want to make sure that you truly understand the weight of this responsibility. These plans may be emailed to you, found in the LMS, or a hard copy placed in your mailbox. You will likely have several to many students with one of these plans. The first thing you need to do is to read through every IEP and create a "cheat sheet" of what you, the teacher, will be responsible for doing. Sometimes a great special education teacher on your team or co-teacher will create this for you, but don't wait for someone to do this for you.

The documents themselves are many pages long, often providing the anecdotal data that will give you some insights into things that have previously worked well for the student and what doesn't. For example, "student responds best to quiet verbal prompts" or "student shuts down when singled out." I'd argue that is true for all students, but you get my point. You will need to determine how assessments will be different for the child.

Do they need extra time? That can be 1.5 time or 2.0 time, and occasionally even more. This means they have to be given one and a half or two times the amount you are allotting for all students to complete the task, without penalty. Do they need breaks? You might need to call a hall monitor to give the child a break if they become distressed. Do they need a copy of class notes? This would mean that you provide a scanned copy of the notes students would typically copy down in class or a hard copy for the child's binder. Sometimes a special education teacher will be helping you, but depending on your district's configuration for special education, it could be more up to you than you'd expect.

I keep a notecard on every student in my class, and I would highly recommend this practice. Depending on the number of students you have, the information can be incredibly overwhelming. I use the largest note cards I can find, and I jot down notes about IEPs, 504s, and information from the surveys I give parents and students. If I learn something new from another source, I jot that down too. These notecards are messy, scrawled in different colored pen, often with coffee rings, but I am confident that approaching all my students as individuals in need of a plan is the best way to provide an educational experience for my students that will help them grow into the best versions of themselves.

Once you get your mind around the accommodations and modifications that you will be providing, it can sometimes be easier to provide it for all students. For example, if I have a student who requires a copy of class notes, I have no problem providing that for all students in our Google Classroom, as that simply requires me to post my slideshow. That is beneficial for all students, and it doesn't create any extra work for me, while meeting that child's needs. I realized this years ago when I regularly emailed my college students copies of slideshows. Why wouldn't I email my students' parents a copy of a slideshow or put it in our Google Classroom? That helps everyone.

If you are invited to attend a 504 or IEP meeting, you are meeting as a part of a committee who decides what this child's educational plan will be. If you attend an "initial determination" meeting, the committee is deciding if the child qualifies for special education or not. Sometimes they will qualify for a 504 with just the accommodations, but in more serious cases they will qualify for an IEP which requires specialized programming. In this "initial determination" meeting it is important to know that you are not truly deciding this child's fate. Instead, you are there to provide anecdotal information and observational data when asked. The student will have gone through a battery of testing, and it is those results that mostly determine a child's placement.

If you are invited to attend an annual review, the child already has a 504 or an IEP, and you are there to determine, with the committee, if the plan is working or needs adjusting in any way. This is where your knowledge of the child is very important. For example, if a child has 1.5 extra time on tests, yet still struggles to complete the assessments, you need to let the committee know that. As a group, you may decide to limit the number of questions on an assessment or to extend the time to 2.0 instead. These meetings sometimes have a parent advocate present, and that is likely because the parent feels uncomfortable arguing for their child's needs and may believe there needs to be more support offered that is not currently happening. Be careful in these situations, as they are sometimes there to gather evidence for legal pursuits.

Your role is to speak to the child's needs in your class. Don't offer suggestions about anything you are unsure of; for example, I, as an ELA teacher, can't presume how long it will take a student to complete a math task. Speak only from your experience with the child. You should be consulting your notecard, data from the LMS (attendance and grades are what you'll need), and data from standardized testing that your district uses (STAR testing or iReady or Aimsweb to name a few). You may not need all of this information, but it is helpful to have with you. As a rule, keep your comments brief, framed positively, and factual. For example, you might say "Johnny always works diligently but doesn't always finish. He wants to do his best, and I think a little more time would help him do that," not "Johnny runs out of time and is irritated by the time limits."

Remember, first and foremost, that this student of yours is their baby, and their baby needs help in this world. You are that help. Consider how difficult it must be to have to fight for your child to have a chance at success that is going to be measured very differently than anyone plans for, and certainly won't be what they'd hoped. If you lean into an empathetic role—going through this journey *with* their child, instead of a sympathetic one where you feel sorry for their child, you will make a profound difference in not only the life of the child, but for their whole family as well.

Pre-conferences

Every teacher, no matter how good or confident, worries about their observations. Schools have a variety of ways they measure teacher success, but an observation is always a part of that evaluation measure, as it should be. You'll likely be notified that your principal, an assistant principal, or some other administrator will be observing you on a particular date at a given time. Some allow you to pick the time, but many do not. Your district will have its only method for this process, but it is crucial that you take this very seriously, while also not panicking.

In your new teachers' handbook or contract or documents drive you will find the rubric that will be used to assess your lesson. Study this! Dissect it and make sure that the lesson you do will have easily identified elements. For example, there's often a standard regarding questioning techniques. Make sure that you are quite overt in how you ask questions, even so far as to say, "Ok folks, let me take some of your questions, and I have a few for you as well."

The pre-conference is your opportunity to explain to your administrator what your lesson is about and what they should expect to see. You should provide them with the lesson plan, a copy of student data (grades, attendance), and I'd suggest a

"What You Need to Know About" sheet. This sheet is where you can put all that data I mentioned before that "really matters." It might look like this:

- Suzy has been on vacation for a week. This is her first day back.
- Johnny's aunt died last week, and he's not taking it well.
- I'm working on getting Missy to participate. She has never spoken in class, and we have a plan for her to try.
- Danny got a 100 for the first time ever last week on a reading quiz. He's very proud of himself.
- Maddie self-harms, and has been struggling lately. We have a cue if she needs a break, so I may call a monitor to take her for a walk.

This "What You Need to Know About" sheet serves many purposes—besides just being a good practice. It helps your admin see that you have knowledge of your learners and care about them, a competency that is on most observational rubrics. It also shows your ability to adapt and differentiate, which is also on most observational rubrics. These are hard to simply observe, but by providing it, you have helped streamline their data about your teaching.

Post-conferences

The lesson is over. You think it went well. The students really rose to the occasion, some definitely better than they've ever behaved! Your administrator will set a post-conference meeting, sometimes a few days later or some even a few weeks later. Immediately after the lesson, jot down anything that stood out to you, both the good and the bad. I once had an administrator who began our post-conference with the question, "What was the best thing that happened in your class today and what would you change?" Talk about loaded questions!

I'll give you this piece of advice: always be student-centered in your answers. Even though it is YOUR observation, and

YOUR future at stake, it is always best to set that aside and focus on what really matters: are students learning and how do you know? I didn't answer his question this way, but if I could go back and do it again, I would have said,

> The best thing that happened in class today was that my students were all engaged in the lesson, even a few I mentioned on the What You Should Know sheet who are struggling. What would I change? I'm not sure I'd change anything, but I'd love your feedback.

It is really important to understand that teaching is an art and a science. It is a balancing act, a comedy routine, and a lesson all rolled into one. Almost every single lesson can be critiqued, and almost every administrator has the things they zero in on. Do not expect to receive the highest ratings in all categories. You shouldn't be an expert in your first years. You can be good, even very good, but you should always approach observations with an eye toward what you can learn. Remember the "comparison is the thief of joy" quote from earlier? Do not discuss your observation with anyone other than your mentor or a close friend, preferably one who doesn't teach. The thing about the observation is that as much as they try to standardize it, it is still subjective.

Should you ever challenge what is written in your observation? I'd say tread lightly, but I'd also say that if there is information that the administrator misunderstood or missed, you should fill them in. I once was observed by an old-school administrator who counted the number of times I called on boys vs. girls. She docked me for calling on girls far more often. In fact, she pointed out, I called on 13 girls and only 5 boys. I was able, carefully, to point out that I only had 5 boys in the class!

Finally, the observation is important, but it isn't all there is to you and your teaching. If an administrator critiques something, find a solution or strategy and ask them to stop back in so that you can show them what you've come up with to improve. Even though you are the teacher, you can learn from every experience.

Disciplinary

I've saved the worst and best meetings for last. A disciplinary meeting is called when you have violated a rule, code, or contractual obligation and the administrator wants to formalize the incident. It usually results in a letter in your personnel file if the situation is deemed fixable and is not a pattern. In school districts without tenure, and even those with it, in your first three years, you can be terminated on the spot. If you are ever summoned to a meeting with an administrator, ask if you should bring representation (if you have a union in your district). If you can bring representation, definitely do so.

You will be very nervous, as you should be, but you have to keep your head. There are ways to make the situation better and some to make it worse. First, consider what the "summons" is about. Most administrators do not tell you why you are being called in, and it is both a power play and a strategy to see how you react. They want to know if you are guilty of the thing they are going to accuse you of, and they don't want you to wiggle out of it if it is truly not acceptable. Let's go down two paths.

Let's pretend you are guilty. You are called down because you lost your cool and swore at a student, and stated "This is why you'll be bagging my groceries." This is definitely unprofessional, but maybe worthy of a letter, or, probably determined by who the child's connections are, an offense worthy of termination. Be humble, contrite, and don't make a single excuse. Don't tell them about this child's ongoing behavior issues, as I'm positive they have already checked into who the child is. Don't tell them about your lack of sleep or stress levels. Apologize, agree to never do anything like that again, and be silent. As a union representative, I've sat in on many of these meetings, and I spend the entire time urging my members to be quiet. Little can be gained from saying too much.

If the writing is on the wall, and they are going to terminate you, you or your representative may ask if instead you can resign. This will be unimaginably important later when you have to answer the question on the application that says, "Have you ever been terminated from a job?" You want to check no to that box, and if you are being terminated there is no reason to be too proud at that moment to ask for mercy. It is crucial that you resign and are not terminated. School districts know that teachers don't typically resign in the middle of the year, so it isn't like you are walking away unscathed. Rather, it is at least still possible to salvage your career, and be sure to request to resign instead.

The second path is tricky. Let's say you didn't do what you are being accused of doing. You will want to make your case, but you want to give the administrator an "out" too. They've called you down, possibly to terminate you, and you are going to try to talk them out of it. Focus on how the situation is a misunderstanding. Let's say that the student who accused you of swearing and insulting them is lying. It becomes a "he said/she said" situation. In this case, you might want to say something like,

> I know that you have to investigate situations like this, and I appreciate the position you are in, but I did not do this. Can I give you the list of students who were in the room at the time, and you can check with some of them?

Be confident, but not cocky. Whatever you do, don't get emotional and say something that will make them think you could have lost your cool.

There's nothing easy about a disciplinary meeting. You either have made a mistake or are accused of doing so. The most important thing you can do in either situation is to be calm, speak reasonably (and very briefly), and do not become defensive. I've seen these meetings go extremely well, and others go terribly. The difference is almost always the demeanor of the accused. Creating a scene of any kind is almost always a ticket out the door, as schools already have enough built in drama without adding to it.

Finally, no matter the outcome, don't breathe a word to anyone. Chances are, someone has already watched you walk in with a union rep, and there will already be some gossip. Nothing in schools is exempt from gossip, unfortunately. However, if you are allowed to resign, the district can rescind that offer if you walk out and start blowing up everyone's phones about it. If you escaped the situation intact, you don't speak of it to anyone. Pretend it never happened. The last thing you want is drama attached to your name, especially if you are vindicated!

Tenure

I'm a proud union President, and I have only worked in unionized schools, so I've lived with the idea of tenure for my whole career. The first time I received tenure it was remarkably unceremonious. I had a slip of yellow paper in my mailbox congratulating me on receiving tenure on a specific date. That was it. No dog and pony show, no portfolio meeting.

The second time I received tenure it was after having to take five Dimensions of Learning classes and do a portfolio presentation for my principal, Assistant Superintendent of Instruction, and Superintendent. It was a big deal with lots of preparation. I didn't know this at the time, but if someone isn't getting tenure, they would probably already have a really good idea from their poor observations, conversations, etc. That doesn't mean that a tenure meeting isn't important, but it does mean that you shouldn't be shocked by either getting tenure or not. Some districts offer an extra year for teachers who they believe have promise, but they don't want to commit to quite yet.

Receiving tenure is, by far, the most coveted part of being a teacher, and the most controversial. Being tenured, despite what some may think, doesn't mean you can't be fired. It means that it is very difficult and expensive to fire you unless you have committed a felony. Those against tenure argue that it protects bad teachers (it does) and those for it say that it allows teachers protection from aggressive parents and disrupter administrators who wish to make sweeping changes on their watch (it does this too). Tenure is a complex conversation, and it is one that is unfortunately more relevant than ever given the political climate.

If you are fortuitous enough to work in a district where tenure is a possibility, jump through every single hoop, take all the classes, and do all the things that would allow you to receive it!

This chapter felt like a whole day of meetings, right? There's so much to know, and it is hard to guess what to expect. Every situation is going to be different, but these pieces of advice will help all educators. Sadly, there are way more meeting types than I describe here. It can become the very thing that sucks the life and passion from your teaching. However, every job has its ups and downs, and there are many things that need to be accomplished to keep a school district moving. Go to the meetings you have to, limit yourself to no more than two committees, and always come prepared. Most importantly, use the time you spend in meetings and on committees ingratiating yourself to the people who will be a part of your life for a very long time. Get to know them. Ask about their families. Remember their likes and dislikes. Bring them a coffee or tea. Bake cookies for the next meeting. When it comes down to it, being a successful teacher in a happy career comes from the environment where you work, and you have the power to make that a positive experience, even as a newbie!

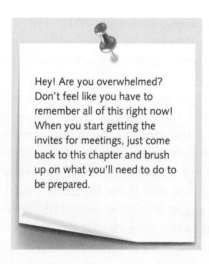

Hey! Are you overwhelmed? Don't feel like you have to remember all of this right now! When you start getting the invites for meetings, just come back to this chapter and brush up on what you'll need to do to be prepared.

Mentoring moment

1. What types of meetings can you expect in your role?
2. Who are the "key players" in each type of meeting? For example, who is the team leader? Is there a department chair? Who runs the data meetings? Prepare for meetings by finding out who is in charge of the meeting. In the first meeting, make observations about how they run it and what they are expecting from you.
3. Do you know the locations of the different types of meetings? Some meetings might not be in your building or in some area you've never been before. Find out where the meetings are, and make sure you give yourself enough time!
4. Will there be parents at the meeting? If so, you might consider dressing up a little more than normal. First impressions matter, and new teachers who are younger will be taken more seriously if you look the part, even if your district has looser requirements.
5. What type of record should you keep for the meeting? Consider having a "meeting notebook" or binder where you keep everything together. Some people have smaller notebooks for each type of meeting.

5

Protecting your peace

During the height of the pandemic in 2020, there was a teacher in our district who worked tirelessly on our Health and Safety Committee. However, when I asked her if she'd continue in this leadership role within our union for the 2021 school year, she declined, using a phrase I'd never heard before: "I need to protect my peace." I loved this as soon as I heard it, though I was going to miss her expertise. Protecting your peace is perhaps the most difficult part of teaching, and it is largely undiscussed. In this chapter, I'm going to share some ways to uphold your values while protecting your peace. As an English teacher, I teach students about all the types of conflict, so I'm going to organize it that way for you.

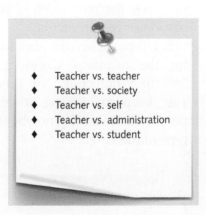

- ◆ Teacher vs. teacher
- ◆ Teacher vs. society
- ◆ Teacher vs. self
- ◆ Teacher vs. administration
- ◆ Teacher vs. student

DOI: 10.4324/9781003365921-5

Teacher vs. teacher

Your school community becomes a family, and in every family there's the "crazy uncle" or the "moody sister." This is true in schools as well. There will be people who get on your last nerve. There will be people who even *dance* on your last nerve. I've found that teachers can go through amazingly difficult situations—like virtual teaching, hybrid teaching, severe weather, and emergencies functioning as a cohesive, unified, group. Yet, just like the little things can bother you in your own house, it can be the day-to-day hassles that will push people over the edge. In my house, it drives me crazy when my family yells from a room that is too far away for anyone to hear. It drives my husband crazy when we let the trash get too full without taking it out, or at least squashing it all down so the lid will shut! My daughter thinks we are all horrible at loading the dishwasher. My son can't believe the way leftovers take over our fridge. Just as we have to learn to live with each others' quirks, habits, and opinions, you'll face the same thing in your building.

As tempting as it may be, as often as you hear other people doing it, do not gossip. Do not talk about anyone behind their backs. Trust me when I tell you, you don't want to deal with the repercussions, especially if you live in a small town or close knit community. That bossy teacher is likely someone's aunt or that ridiculously loud music teacher is married to a teacher in another building who is BFFs with the teacher you just complained to. For example, in my district, I know of at least three sets of teachers who are married. I know of four children of teachers who work in the district. There are several siblings who work together here. The wrong off-handed comment could spread fast, even out of your building. Besides being tacky, it is also a dealbreaker for most districts if they hear there is a troublemaker amongst the ranks.

Let me give it to you from a Human Resources position. If two employees are bickering, or someone brings your gossip to their attention, they could be required to investigate if you are creating a hostile work environment or if what you said could be construed as harassing. Even if you are just "piling on" to what someone else said, you could become a part of a really sticky situation. These investigations are time-consuming, and in the end, Human Resources should not have your name on their mind! If it comes down to an untenured or new teacher who can be scapegoated, it just might happen because disciplining a tenured employee becomes a union issue, which most districts try to avoid.

I'm sure this sounds a bit dramatic, but I've seen firsthand how a building can turn against a new teacher. Every building has its own homeostatic environment, and when a new teacher is introduced, there's a period of either assimilation or rejection. If you "fit' the building, you'll be welcomed in, but if you seem like poison, they have no patience for helping you grow as a teacher. Teachers who would turn on you aren't evil or heartless; instead, they are protecting their environment from what they perceive as a poison that could be very contagious.

My advice is to be an expert people watcher. *Observe the relationships that exist, be humble, and find your "people," the ones who take an interest in you and go out of their way to make you feel comfortable.* Find your allies and you could begin one of the lifetime friendships I've mentioned. I consider myself to be incredibly fortunate to have found a work family who has supported me through the complexities of life, from having babies, to mourning deaths, to celebrating my kiddos' successes and comforting me when I'm overwhelmed. There are no friends better than teacher work friends. You need each other, so even if you are tempted, never air any of your complaints to anyone who works with you. If you must, tell your significant other, or a good friend!

Teacher vs. society

The pandemic, politics, and fear have brought out sides of "society" that I didn't know existed. I put society in quotes because it is hard in a digital, connected, global era to pinpoint what that word means. As I've explained when I talked about social media, it is hard sometimes as a teacher to not get sucked into online drama. This is not to say that you shouldn't have an online professional presence. I encourage that. However, "society" already has some conceptions of what our profession is like. When I tell people I teach middle school, they usually say, "Oh. I could never. That must be a draining job. God bless you!" Then, when it is my summer vacation, the same people say, "Must be nice to have a two month vacation!" My answer to both is "Yes—to both. It is incredibly draining and it is nice to have a two month vacation," though I never try to explain what my daughter and I call the "teacher life."

My daughter Zoey is going to college next fall to become a teacher. She's loved teaching (and being the "boss") since she was three years old, reading to her infant brother and narrating our entire life. She'd sit in the backseat with him, explaining, "This is how we go to church. We will be going to lunch after." Recently, we were chatting about her career choice, and she said something so interesting to me. She said, "I want to be a teacher, but I can't imagine not having the 'teacher life.'" I knew what she meant, but she went on,

> I want to have room in my life to be an adjunct professor or write or travel. I need to be home with my family over school breaks. I want to go on adventures every day in the summer like we did. I can't imagine not living like our life.

You don't need to apologize for your career choice, amount of holidays, or anything else. There will be people who tell you how much more money you could make in another career based on the amount of college you have finished. The "teacher life" is also things like working two or three jobs in your first years in order to survive. It is also going to school when you are mentally and physically drained. It is sacrificing nights to your piles of paperwork (more about that below). The "teacher life" is a good life, and for some of us, all we've ever known. I went to kindergarten at five years old and have never had a fall when I didn't go to school, either to be a student or be the teacher.

Society can tell you who you are supposed to be, but only you know who you are as a teacher, a part of your identity that will evolve through the years. One of the important lessons about society that I hope you'll absorb from reading this book is that you don't have to be a stereotype. I don't give homework, I wear jeans often, I have my nose pierced and tattoos, and I never take the business of teaching middle schoolers too seriously. Some of society would find me refreshing, but I've met some people who have plenty to say about how I'm doing this "teacher life" all wrong. According to them, I'm not pushing students hard enough because I don't grade them for responsibility. Others say that students will never learn if I let them revise everything they do. Both of those positions—grading students only on the standard, not on how much support they may or may not have at home, and always allowing students to revise and revisit as long as they are learning—are both crucial to me. I've picked my positions that I'm willing to fight for, but I let the rest of the critiquing roll off my back.

Spend some time thinking about what issues—either educational, political, or social that you are willing to take a stand on. You need to find your non-negotiables, and realize that your identity as a teacher depends on how you present yourself to the world. For example, in my career, I've advocated heavily for students in poverty, LGTQIA+ students, and marginalized groups, with an emphasis on SEL. I've been attacked for those affiliations, but it is worth it to me. Be prepared that some of your social justice ideals will come under fire, and you need to consider how you will respond.

In my training as a union President, I've learned that off the cuff remarks are frequently misrepresented, so be wary of offering comments that you don't provide in writing. Some districts frown upon teachers commenting on any situation that the district is involved with, and some outright ban it. You should check your contract to determine how much leeway you have to express your opinions about the district you work for. You might be thinking that this violates your free speech, but when you sign your contract, if it says you can't talk to the press or comment on school matters, then you have sacrificed your free speech for a steady paycheck.

I remember there was a scandal of some sort when I taught high school, and a reporter reached out to me, promising me anonymity for an "insider's view" of the situation. I doubt I would have said anything, but I had a street smart husband who told me to hang up the phone. No good was going to come from something like that. In your own Tweets, Facebook and Instagram posts, it is never a bad thing to have a disclaimer like "Tweets are my own" or "Posts are my opinions," as you don't want to be accused of answering for your district. Be sure that you are staying within the confines of your contract.

In my role as union president, I always caution our members to be very careful appearing critical of the district on social media. If you are a tenured teacher, you have a bunch more latitude, but I'll still caution that derogatory comments on social media often end up being shared with Human Resources, the Board of Education, or the Superintendent. Again, when comparing the district to a family, consider this: It's often ok if you make a comment about your family like "Our family is addicted to drama" but imagine if you read somewhere "that family is addicted to drama." Somehow, we can always talk crap about our own family but when someone else does it becomes fighting words!

Teacher vs. self

Your harshest critic is probably going to be yourself. It is hard to have perspective when you are in the thick of things. As a new teacher, you have so much to learn and will make mistakes. All of us have been there. I once thought Wednesday spirit day was pajama day. It was not. I showed up in my full pajamas, slippers, and bathrobe to be met with students and teachers wearing their sports gear. I felt like an idiot, and my mistake showed what a rookie I was. Now, I know that pajama day is always the last day of spirit week, on a Friday. You have to learn to laugh, or you'll cry. *I always tell teachers I mentor that every year has a rhythm to it, and they'll find it, but they shouldn't expect to understand it until they've had a chance to listen to the whole song first.* I believe that you could put me in a classroom, and based on my observations, I could tell you which month it was—that's how predictable school will become, but in the beginning, you are having to learn everything. You need to know the tune before you can harmonize.

Teacher mom alert—this next piece of advice is critical and a bit naggy. Take care of yourself. I don't know many new teachers who don't spend Thanksgiving in bed sick. Why? It's the first time their body has let down its defenses, and they've worn themselves out. You need to learn to listen to the signs and give your body what it needs! Stress does a number on you too, so make sure that if you need an objective outsider to help with the emotional rollercoaster that you find a good therapist or counselor. Remember that your whole life isn't teaching. You need to make time for your friends, family, and significant others.

The problem with this advice is that you'll need to find your own "teacher life" that makes sense to you. For my first several years, I brought home a whole lot of work, and I had to plan as I went. It won't stay the same because as your life changes, so too will your ability to juggle it all. It was when I had children that I stopped bringing work home. I don't socialize much at school, and I work straight through my day. As new teachers, some of you will be in Masters' programs, and many of you will be working a second job. You need to remember that you don't have limitless reserves. I talk about this in *The Flexible SEL Classroom*. People can generally keep five balls in the air at a time without sacrificing quality.

It's almost Christmas, and I know that the five balls I'm juggling today are: my daughter, my son, entertaining my students the day before break, shopping, and preparing for an impending blizzard. My husband and I just agreed to exchange Christmas on New Year's Eve because we haven't shopped for each other. We dropped the "marriage" ball, but luckily, we've been married a long time and it will work out just fine, and we are excited to shop the sales next week! What other balls am I dropping right now? Health. I just ate three Christmas cookies because all of my care and concern are directed elsewhere. What else? I am not going to grade the test my students took yesterday. It will just have to wait.

I'm telling you all of this because you have to have some grace for yourself. You don't have to be perfect at anything, but you will be better at everything if you only keep five (or maybe six) balls in the air at the same time. If you have too many things that are dividing your attention, you will lose sight of the juggle and drop the ball on something really important. This week I had a really important meeting that I had to attend. No matter what, that had to be one of the balls I juggled. I had to put one of the others down, and all of them are important! This complicated juggle will impact what kind of "teacher life" you create.

Teacher vs. administrator

Occasionally, I'll have a teacher tell me that an administrator doesn't like them, or visa versa. I almost always find that it isn't a like or dislike conflict but rather an awkwardness. Maybe you were never formally introduced, and you think the adminis-trator ignores you. That same administrator could have a hard time remembering names, and it's awkward to ask. Maybe when the administrator walked past your room, and you were on your cell phone, he kept going so as to not interrupt. You may then be paranoid that he thinks you're on your phone too much. The fact is, people really hate awkward. If you find yourself in this type of situation, honesty and candor go a long way.

I also remind new teachers that it is easy to be paranoid when so much is riding on your success. The pressure to be a good teacher—or even a great one—is profound, and it can make a person question everything. The best way to know if the issue you are feeling is "real" or if it your fear getting in the way is to pay attention. Does the administrator stop into lots of other peoples' rooms and purposely avoid yours? Or, after closer attention do you find that this particular administrator isn't big on disturbing teachers in their own space? You can create some very unfortunate self-fulling prophecies if you allow your fear to dictate your vision.

This is not to say that administrators don't have favorites. They absolutely do. Just like everyone else, they have egos, they have the need to be liked, and they too are under the watchful eye of the public. Teachers who make them look good, work with them whenever possible, and are reliable generally do garner favor vs. teachers who rabble rouse, are adversarial or aren't reliable. This is common sense. Some people go into teaching with the impression that it will all be fair. It won't. Some people are going to have advantages. For example, in our community, many administrators are former teachers for our district. They know people. They have history with people. They often went to school together. These scenarios breed relationships which in turn create a work environment that might be different than yours will be just starting out.

I'm often accused of receiving favoritism as our union President. Part of that perception is that my role contractually affords me things that other teachers don't have. Part of that perception is that my role is very political and much of the external niceties are just that: I have to go toe to toe with administrators to negotiate our contract, defend teachers, and advocate for better working conditions. On the flip side, these administrators know that we will all get more of what we want if we work together and toward mutually agreeable outcomes. To create a "win/win" scenario, I'm often navigating tricky situations.

I've been president for three terms now, so most teachers know this and respect that I'm always working for my teachers, but a newbie to our district might wonder why I'm leaving early (almost always to go to a meeting), or why I talk with administrators so much. Be careful not to make assumptions about administrator and teacher relationships, as teachers also serve as coaches, department chairs, and the like, which requires a nuanced relationship. If an administrator isn't as friendly as you'd like, it might simply be that your role as a new teacher has to evolve over time. They are weighing out if you are a good hire or not, and they might be keeping their distance until they have a better idea.

However, unfortunately, there are times when the conflict isn't a perception but a difficult reality. Maybe it is deserved. Maybe you dropped a ball that you shouldn't have, leaving them in an untenable situation with parents or their higher ups. In that case, I recommend that you accept responsibility, apologize, and then work on reconstructing your reputation. Pay extra attention to deadlines, show up early and stay late (not unreasonably so, but appearances do matter), and more than anything else, focus your attention on your students, and you have a chance to redeem yourself.

Sometimes the conflict is justified from your side. Maybe the administrator singles you out, harasses you, or has simply decided they don't want you in their building. You have a few choices, but none of them are easy. You can stay and hope to ride out the situation, and maybe the administrator will change their opinion or move on to someone else. You can look for opportunities within your district to transfer to a new building, but this is often based on seniority. Finally, you can start to look for another position. This is your last resort, but employers can read between the lines. Resigning a position is better by far than losing your job or not receiving tenure. You will need to think about the narrative you'll need to craft that will help you.

Resigning is obviously a last ditch effort, but it is a crucial move if you want to stay local. The best thing you can do is to go to your principal and discuss the resignation, thanking them for the opportunity, but acknowledge that this is not a great fit. Offer to stay until they can find a replacement for you or finish out a semester or the year. Let them know that you have learned from your experiences at the school, and that you hope that they'd be willing to support your employment in a new district. In this way, you have solved a big problem they have: they have chosen you, who they no longer think is a "good hire." Instead of having to admit that, you can resign and part more amicably.

Just as teachers across districts know one another, so too do district administrators. You can't expect to go into an interview and say, "My last principal was a bully" or "My principal was out to get me." This could be 100% true, but you run the risk of getting blacklisted as a difficult teacher. Instead, think about potential positives of working in the new district. Focus your attention there. For example, perhaps you were driving a half hour to work in the old district, and the one you are interviewing at is right around the corner from your house. You might say something like, "I really like to participate in my schools' activities, and District A was a pretty long commute for me. I feel like I'll be more effective in a school that is in my community."

Maybe you are willing to switch grade bands. You can say something like, "I realized that early elementary wasn't a good fit for me. My strengths are better suited for 4th and 5th grade. I'd love to explore how I can serve students in this district." This allows everyone to save face. If you've remained professional, your chances of a fresh start are much better. Don't beat yourself up too much, but really spend some time debriefing with a trusted educator and analyze what you will do differently the next time around. Own what is yours, but you can also accept that not all jobs are created equally! Some districts are far superior to others in terms of their job satisfaction, and that is outside of your control.

Teacher vs. student and caregiver

I've saved the most complicated conflict until last. It may be complicated, but the answer is simple: **you are the adult** and must never, ever pick up the rope. It is a tug of war that you will ALWAYS lose. A student can call you names, get in your face, walk out of your room, spread rumors about you, and generally make your life hell, but you can not retaliate. You can't call them names, get in their face, walk out of your room, or speak about the child at any time. You will ALWAYS lose. **You are the adult**.

This is a really complicated conflict because we are all human. A student may push all our buttons, but we must absolutely remain in control of the situation. The main way new teachers find themselves in hot water is poor behavior management that leads to unwinnable situations with students. No matter how irritated you may be, you can't pick up the rope. It is a no-win for you. Your role is to be a trusted, calm, and respected adult in your classroom. Losing your temper, allowing students to see you fall apart, or giving up the authority of your classroom to students is the biggest mistake you can make.

Instead, you must develop from the first minute your students walk in, an "authority of care." This is an attitude that has nothing to do with who they are, but everything to do with who you are. You need to view yourself as THE adult who will be on their side, and THE person who will advocate for their needs. Present yourself that way, and you will find that when you radically care for students, things will fall into place. What does this look like?

First, you need to simply identify for them what your role is in their lives. There are different kinds of teachers, so you need to spell it out. This is what I say to my 8th graders on the first day of school:

> I remember how difficult middle school can be, and I want to let you know that I am on your side. If you need someone to talk to, I hope it will be me. If you need someone to defend you, I will. If you have anything that needs an adult to handle, please let me help you. I am here to be your ELA teacher, but it is more important to me to help you be the best person you can be. I will help you, whatever it takes. Please know that if you are ever rude or disrespectful to me or our class community, I will call you out. I will tell you that you are hurting my feelings or those of your classmates. We have to count on each other in this room. Middle school can suck, but in this room, you are allowed to be yourself and we will learn together. You may think I'm a ridiculous lady up here, but I promise you that I will not change, no matter what you do. I will care for you and take care of you. That's my biggest job.

If you think this speech gets a rousing round of applause, you haven't been inside a middle school.

What I get are smirks, head shakes, eye rolls, and even some laughter. But every single day, I show up with that mantra (simplified to "whatever it takes") and eventually they believe me. Eventually, after I write a late pass because their next teacher will freak out if they are late, or if I have a granola bar for them, or if I give them grace when they say something stupid (they will), they believe me. Once that happens, any conflict I could have is protected by the community we've created together. Here's an example that happened just last week, keeping in mind that it was the week before Christmas break.

I was trying to help them review for our *The Outsiders* test. I knew that about 15 to 20 of my 110 hadn't read the entire book or listened to the audio. I knew those students had no chance of passing the test. Some others had struggled because one of the major post-pandemic trends I've noticed is my students' really low stamina. This was the first book that some of my students have been asked to read outside of class, on their own, in their entire middle school career. I don't blame their teachers, as I wouldn't want to be held to my teaching ideals during the last three years either. We were all doing our best. When kiddos struggle, they act out, deflect, and want to make their poor performance be about anything (even bad behavior) rather than their deficiency. In each class, I had a few students disrupting each class. So, here's what I said:

> All right everyone. I'm seeing some attitudes and behaviors that aren't working for our class. I know that some of you didn't read and some didn't read all of it. You are probably going to fail this test tomorrow, but you are causing problems for those who need to study. Do me a favor? Take the test. Do your best. But, over break, go on to our Google Classroom and listen to the audio or read the book. You're going to need to overcome the fact that you didn't have the stamina to do the work. I'm offering you a safety net. You can fix your problem by reading over break and taking a test then. Can we agree that this was really hard? (Head's nod) Can we agree that some people worked really hard and deserve this review? (Head's nod) Can you allow me to help them? I'm giving you another chance and grace. I care about all of you and will help you, but you need to let me help those who need it today. Please respect that.

The disruptive behaviors stopped. I radically cared about my students. I didn't write them off when they didn't meet my expectations. I didn't leave them with no options of doing well. They knew I was right. When someone started chatting instead of listening, I was able to ask, "Can I help you with something else?" The class knows I mean it. When they know that you are the adult who will not be deterred from caring for and about them, and are willing to help them be successful, they will not enter into conflict with you. If they try, **you are the adult**, and you can redirect them to work toward being a part of the class community. Since I've adopted this "authority of care," I've stopped the conflicts that could happen with students.

To make this approach even more transformational, I include families and caregivers, and let the principals, assistant principals, and guidance counselors know that this is my philosophy. I use the same ridiculously, radically caring language. If a student steps out of line, I help them find their way back, without judgment. I email parents when their child is struggling and offer grace and a helping hand. The conflict with families has stopped as well. A caregiver who believes that you are truly a non-judgmental partner in helping their child will always support you.

You might wonder why I didn't have a separate section about conflict with caregivers. The answer is this: any conflict you have with a child is a conflict with their caregiver, and the same is true in reverse. Any conflict you have with a caregiver is a conflict with the child. You have to take the child and their family, as they are. As a mom, there is absolutely no way that you can critique my child without critiquing me. My child's conflict with a teacher becomes my conflict. The way to handle this symbiotic relationship is to recognize its power. If I have words with a student, I let the family know. We all need to work together to help the child. I've had to give students a failing grade, and families know that we did our best together. I've had to write a referral that a student will surely be suspended for, but the family, administrators, and the child knows that I will do everything I can to help them.

I do have a few suggestions that help make working together with caregivers more effective:

- ◆ Communicate in the way they want. I have parents fill out a survey, and they provide me with a phone number to call (and I offer them the option for me to text), an email, or a note in their child's agenda or folder.
- ◆ Just like you wouldn't want to be judged on your very worst lesson, don't judge a caregiver who overreacts.

Give them space, grace, and an opportunity to work
things out.

◆ Never assume that caregivers are not interested in their
kiddo's well-being if they don't respond to you right
away (or even at all). We don't know what their past
experiences of school are, and for some people a judg-
mental teacher is always looming in their minds. Many
caregivers are also "cleaning up the mess" of their
children's lives by raising grandkids, nieces, nephews, or
siblings and might not want their dirty laundry aired for
everyone. Give everyone the benefit of believing in their
interest in the student.

◆ Finally, we all know that the stories they hear about us
aren't likely all 100% true. Remember that when they
make an accusation or only know part of the story. We
are the adults. We can sort it out!

Conflict is a part of life. We aren't always going to get along with
everyone, and we must learn to protect our peace. We do this by
identifying our non-negotiables and figuring out what kind of
"teacher life" we want, and then you fight for that. There are some
parts of teaching that you can't control, and there are so many
relationships that must be navigated. For example, I have 100
teachers in my building, and I work closely with about a dozen
of them. I have two assistant principals and a principal. I have
110 students with probably 200 caregivers (parents, step parents,
grandparents, and guardians). There are two counselors, one
social worker, and one school psychologist who are partners in
caring for my students. Unless you commit yourself to a mantra
of who you are, it is too easy to fall into squabbles and petty
arguments. Teaching requires a dedication to your philosophical
position, and then you have to lean into whatever it takes to live
that life. For me, I promise to have an "authority of care" that will
help my students to navigate middle school and become the best
version of themselves. Anything else that happens is secondary
to that goal, and as long as it doesn't impede them, I let things go.

This chapter was heavy on philosophy, but I think it is
important to know your why. Teaching is too hard to do as a job.

There are plenty of other careers that will take less out of you. However, teaching is a calling and a life, and if you view it that way, you will do everything you can to rest in that peace, that you are doing your best, and you will protect that at all costs.

Mentoring moment

1. What might you do to avoid conflict with teachers you work with? What specifically about your personality might "grate" on another? Is there a way to neutralize that?
2. What hot button issues do you feel you have to stand up for, no matter the consequence? What protections can you put into place that will separate your actions from your profession? Do you need a disclaimer with your social media?
3. Are you hard on yourself? If so, about what? If not, how are you avoiding the comparison trap? What can you do to protect your peace and give yourself grace?
4. What are your administrators like? How will you interact with them in a professional way? Is there anything you need to work on that might impact your relationship? (Organization, relationships with others, communication, etc.)
5. How can you share your philosophy with your students and their caregivers? How can you build relationships with both?

6

Plan like Dora the explorer

My daughter Zoey is going to graduate high school in a few short months, and I'm fairly certain that much of her success in life is as a result of her early love of Dora the Explorer. If you've ever watched Dora, you'd know that Dora is always going somewhere, always making a plan, and always consults the Map who is stowed carefully away in the side pocket of her ever-present Backpack. Dora is kind of like a traveling party of intellectual curiosity, often stopping for snacks and finding friends along the way, which is pretty much my daughter in a nutshell. As I write this, she's spending the first days of our Winter Break in Dearborn, Michigan on a mission trip where she's sent me pictures of, you guessed it, interesting food she's trying (the latest being a hot cheese dessert which she found questionable) and the new friends she's making along the way.

The truth is though, behind the freewheeling, carefree version of my daughter, there's also been a lot of planning. She wrote letters, asking for support. She researched the community she was going to, and she's been attending meetings for months to prepare. We've thrifted clothing that will help her ingratiate herself respectfully into the community she's going to. She's been reading constantly. The truth is, she's been mapping out what she wants from this trip for a long time, so though she is going to have new, fresh experiences, she's also prepared for them.

DOI: 10.4324/9781003365921-6

Now, of course, life isn't this simple, but the base wisdom of "I'm the Map" from Dora the Explorer is a great reminder for new teachers: with a map, there can be a plan, and with a plan, you can "get where you want to get." The Map always gives Dora directions in sequential order, with a series of steps, which Dora checks off as she gets there. If you are hoping that I'm going to give you your very own map, you'd be halfway correct. However, in this very long metaphor here, you have to create the map because we are all carrying different backpacks with different destinations. Thanks for sticking with me on this one. I promise it makes complete sense!

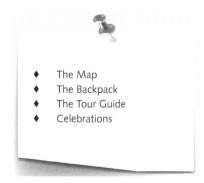

- The Map
- The Backpack
- The Tour Guide
- Celebrations

The map

Of course, as teachers, when we hear the word "map," we think "curriculum map." When it comes down to planning what content you'll be teaching, this is very likely the place where you should start. Your department chair, curriculum coordinator, or principal should provide you with a curriculum map that will lay out for you the scope and sequence of what you will be teaching. These are often posted on websites and aligned to state standards, essentially taking the guesswork out of *what* you'll teach. Sometimes there's a program to be followed, other times, there's a guide, but more than you'd expect, there isn't a handy map with *how* you'll teach the content. But, before we talk about the *how*, we have to embrace our role as mapmaker—cartographers of the classroom!

Journal Topics

For each entry due, choose one or two of the topics/questions to discuss in 2 to 3 paragraphs. Double-spaced, 12-point font, "formal" writing expectations. This is practice! **Each journal entry will count as a 10-point classwork grade. You will be exempted from ONE. However, these only receive ½ credit if they are late since you should be doing them during class time.**

You will do one final short answer (2 paragraphs) question that you'll answer about your book in class that will count as a final test grade. I'll give you that question later, but you should use a notecard or create a file of quotes that are related to CHARACTERIZATION. Remember how difficult it was to write *The Outsiders* paper and find the quotes? Keep track of your quotes this time!

Final reminders:

- 2 complete paragraphs, no less than 5 sentences each
- Run through Grammarly
- You must do 7 out of 8 entries. However, they are due on the due date or they receive ½ credit. Save your "skip" for when you are sick or it is an emergency.
- If you do all 8 entries, 5 points will be added to your final short answer. You can not get over a 100.
- If you finish the first book, you will go get another one :)

Class expectations:

This is a very quiet month. You are practicing your skills and gaining stamina. If you choose not to work or read, that is up to you. If you distract anyone, I will intervene. You may listen to your book, but you must read along as well.

Journal #1

A) What are you learning in the exposition of your book?

B) What do you believe is the central conflict that is emerging?

C) Tell me about the PETS of the book.

D) Is your protagonist reliable? (Do you think they are capable of telling the truth?)

FIGURE 6.1

Journal #2

A) What POV is the author using to tell this story? Do you think that it is effective? Or, would you rather have a different POV? Why?

B) At this point, what do you think your protagonist's motivation is? What is making them do what they are doing/ trying to accomplish, etc?

C) Who (or what) is the antagonist of the story? How do you know? Is the antagonist at all likable or have redeeming qualities? Describe them.

D) Do a little research on the author. What do you find out? Cite your source and don't cut and paste. Is anything relevant to the story?

Journal #3

A) Describe a "sidekick" character or friend of the protagonist. What do you think their purpose is in the story? Would you be friends with someone like them?

B) Study the author's style. Think about long and short sentences. Figurative language. Organization of the story (sequential, flashbacks, foreshadowing, shifting narrators, etc). Is there specialized vocabulary or slang that the author is using?

C) Choose a few sentences of dialog and copy it at the top of your paper. Then, explain what is important about the dialog and its contribution to the story.

D) Choose any prompt from Journal 1 that you have not completed. Apply the prompt to THIS chunk of the book though (Don't write about the first few pages for this journal, for example).

Journal #4

A) Is there a villain? If so, what is his/her need that isn't being met that makes them the villain? Could the villain and the protagonist ever unite?

B) Is your character on a journey of some sort? If so, could it also be metaphorical? Watch the video on the hero's journey and decide if this might fit your character. If so, how? If not, why not?

C) How would this story be different if it were told from a different perspective? Really think about this. Which character's perspective would change everything for the book? Why might the author have created that character?

D) Choose any prompt from Journal 1 or Journal 2 that you have not completed. Apply the prompt to THIS chunk of the book though (Don't write about the first few pages for this journal, for example).

FIGURE 6.1 (*Continued*)

Journal #5

A) What symbols are emerging? What do they represent? Why might the author have included them? Watch the symbolism video to better understand the question.

B) What is the time period of the book? Why is this important? What details are provided by the author to create a "rich" atmosphere that feels realistic?

C) Is there a theme emerging? Remember that theme is a sentence that reveals to the reader an important idea or truth that they want us to know. You write it as a SENTENCE. Share the theme that you think is starting to emerge and then share your thoughts on it.

D) Choose any prompt from Journal 1, Journal 2, or Journal 3 that you have not completed. Apply the prompt to THIS chunk of the book though (Don't write about the first few pages for this journal, for example).

Journal #6

A) Think about the main conflict of the story. What type is it (watch the video to figure that out)? What is it that is causing the conflict? What would need to happen/ change/ be accomplished for the conflict to end? Do you see that happening?

B) What is going on in your character's head? (Don't choose this one if you can't/ don't know) Does it match up with the impression you have of the character already? Is there anything out of character?

C) What worries your character? What do you think is driving his or her decisions? Do you worry about the same things?

D) Choose any prompt from Journal 1, Journal 2, Journal 3, or Journal 4 that you have not completed. Apply the prompt to THIS chunk of the book though (Don't write about the first few pages for this journal, for example)

FIGURE 6.1 (*Continued*)

Journal #7

A) Have you reached the climax of your story yet? If not, where is the story headed? Make a prediction. If so, what was it? Was it what you expected? Why or why not?

B) How do you feel about your character? Would you be friends with them? Would you trust them? What makes you have these answers?

C) Does your character's physical appearance (looks in the STEAL method) impact the story in any way? How? Explain.

D) Choose any prompt from Journal 1, Journal 2, Journal 3, Journal 4, or Journal 5 that you have not completed. Apply the prompt to THIS chunk of the book though (Don't write about the first few pages for this journal, for example)

Journal #8

A) You are nearing the end of your book. Is the author starting to "wrap things up"? What loose ends are left? What do you think will happen?

B) What effect has the protagonist had on other characters in the story? (This is the E of the STEAL method)

C) Is this a plot driven book or something else? Is it mostly about feelings, relationships, and interactions or is it dependent on big plot points? Think about the difference between those types of books. Which do you prefer?

D) Choose any prompt from Journal 1, Journal 2, Journal 3, Journal 4, Journal 5, or Journal 6 that you have not completed. Apply the prompt to THIS chunk of the book though (Don't write about the first few pages for this journal, for example)

Extra Credit AFTER finishing

A) What is the resolution to the story? Is this a satisfying ending or not? Why? Explain.

B) Is there room for a sequel or next book in the series? How do you know? Would you read it? Explain either of your answers to that question.

C) Browse some reviews of the book online. Then, write your own review. Try to mimic the style/ language/ organization of the review.

D) Choose any prompt from Journal 1, Journal 2, Journal 3, Journal 4, Journal 5, Journal 6, or Journal 7 that you have not completed. Apply the prompt to THIS chunk of the book though (Don't write about the first few pages for this journal, for example)

FIGURE 6.1 (*Continued*)

We must see who is on the journey with us—our students and their families—and then we must customize their experience. Sure, we have to follow the curriculum map, but we are the ones who are the tour guides, making decisions about what we focus on along the way. We are in charge of the pit stops, detours, and scenic overlooks. As the teacher, you must be prepared to make those decisions without the approval of anyone else because so often they happen spontaneously in the classroom, or as with me and my co-teacher, one of us has a "crazy" idea on the ride into school. If you are discussing character traits, as I once was, and someone says, "bitchy," you sure as heck better be ready to talk about connotation, denotation, and in this case, I even went on a tangent about reappropriation. If your co-teacher sees an inspirational video when she can't sleep at 4 a.m. it makes perfect sense to change your warm-up for the day.

In addition to being the tour guide, you need to realize that you will be, at some point in your career, called upon to be a mapmaker—probably multiple times. For me, I have had to map out what I was going to do for the days after 9/11 when my district was near enough to Boston to have students directly impacted. There's nothing on the curriculum map for that one. I had to make my own map when I cried in front of my class. I've had to make my own map when a class has gone horribly wrong, and so will you. We've all had to make our own map for Zoom meetings, Google calls, "asynchronous" and "hybrid" and all the other made up names used to describe how we were supposed to be educating students during a global pandemic. My map for that catastrophe was simply to show up, take an interest, teach what I could, but show love and kindness in all the ways I hoped students would remember. I delivered Easter baskets to front porches of students who I knew would not have one. I mailed postcards to students every week. We did silly stuff on Zoom calls, and we introduced our pets, and our map veered off into a direction we didn't expect, but as the teacher you have the honor and privilege of not only following maps, but making them too.

The backpack

This bare bones map that we're given as teachers isn't enough. Districts don't typically provide the training on *how* they want you to teach. This is probably a good thing, but when beginning the adventure of teaching it can feel very overwhelming to look at the map and not know how to get from point A to point B, all while knowing that the real goal is to get to point Z. No where are we told strategies, provided tools, or tricks. We aren't Dora, who gets to beckon "Backpack" and get the perfect help suited for the particular adventure. Or are we?

I'd like to suggest that we can, indeed, have a backpack of tips, tricks, and strategies. It won't come pre-loaded with all the things we will need, but we can fill one ourselves. First and foremost, you need to consider where you are going. Are you going to be doing remediation? Acceleration? Both? What climate are you traveling to? Urban? Suburban? Rural? Will you be making this journey alone, or will you travel with a co-teacher? Is there a strong tour guide or were you simply handed the map and told to figure it out? It matters very much that you know where you are going in order to prepare.

For example, next year I'll be teaching a brand new course called "Exploratory Honors English" to two of my 8th grade classes, and I'll have an Integrated Co-teaching (ICT) situation for three of my classes with an average of seven special education students per class. These are going to be very different courses by design, but at the end of 8th grade, all students will take the same proficiency exam. How will I differentiate their experiences? There are some books that I am confident belong in both "backpacks." I want all students to read *The Outsiders* and *The Giver*. However, I'll be adding an SAT prep style vocabulary component to the Honors class, as well as a novel that will let me do a deep dive into the complexities of historical fiction to explore bias and lenses of interpretation. In the Honors backpack, I'll be integrating cross-curricularly, so I need some short nonfiction pieces that compliment the reading.

In the ICT backpack, I'm going to need some materials, tools, and tricks that will help me differentiate for the more diverse population of students. ICT in my district means that I am the lead teacher, but I will have a special education teacher who will co-teach with me, with an emphasis on accommodating and modifying for the special education students in the room. The ICT class will be using iReady, an adaptive program that will shore up students reading who are on or near grade level while filling gaps for those whose reading levels are several grades below. My co-teacher will use the data to create small group reading instruction based on need.

Both backpacks need computers, highly engaging resources, and a destination. While one part of the journey for all of my students is to be successful on the final exam, another portion is to prepare them for high school, and yet another segment is to help them become fully actualized humans who are expanding their understanding of themselves and the world around them. In case you haven't figured this out just yet, these backpacks are heavy!

However, having the right backpack for the situation is one of the most important plans you can make. If I were to throw SAT prep vocabulary at my ICT class, or expect them to annotate and respond to a primary source about the French Revolution while reading *The Queen's Court: Rebel Rose* (a novel about what happens after *Beauty and the Beast*) and then analyze Leo (the Beast) and how he is characterized as experiencing Post-Traumatic Stress, they'd sink. I'd have behavior issues because the content was not accessible to them. Though some educators miss this, the students with higher skills would also become behavior issues if I were to insist on doing reading instruction if they are testing at 10th or 11th grade levels.

There are different backpacks for different situations, but the key to a successful journey with any class is having accessible materials. Additionally, there are those "tips" and "tricks" and strategies, but where can you find those without spending your whole paycheck on Teachers' Pay Teachers? I ask this a little flippantly because I had a mentee who was spending upwards of $25 a week on resources!

My go-to resource is ShareMyLesson because it is vetted by the American Federation of Teachers. The materials will never be sexist, racist, problematic, or of poor quality, and they are all free. Full-disclosure: after becoming a super sharer and posting over 300 lessons on the site, I became a "partner." Am I being paid? Nope. I just have a pretty partner page about me. Their other partners provide quality content as well, often specialized for specific kinds of backpacks. For example, their collections include Black History Month Lesson Plans and Resources, Supporting Safe Schools, Career Exploration, Classroom Management, Restorative Practices, and hundreds more. These collections include webinars on demand, as well as live virtual conferences twice a year.

Teachingchannel.com allows teachers to subscribe and have access to over 1500 classroom videos, filmed in and curated in classrooms around the world, providing real footage of best practices. This isn't free, but my mentee would have benefitted from a year of access for what she was paying TPT. Please don't get me wrong. I am clearly all about teacher entrepreneurship, and I have purchased items before. But, I do see new teachers who are blowing a ton of their tiny paychecks purchasing materials that they could find for free or create themselves. Many districts do not allow teachers to use materials purchased from TPT to be posted on Google Classroom or other student management systems because it will go against the copyright. I've watched new teachers find this out the hard way, and it just isn't worth it.

Edutopia.com is free and has specialized sections by topic, number of years teaching, or grade levels. Their videos are amazing, and I challenge you to check out their collections for inspiration. I've used their videos in my Canisius College "Intro to Differentiation" class to demonstrate some of the "tricks of the trade" that my students might like to try that I myself don't use. When one of my students who teaches elementary school wanted to create a buddy system for reading, I shared the "Developing Literacy Through Reading Buddies" video with her.

As a final exam for my classes at Canisius, I don't test my students on what I taught them. Instead, they are asked to curate their own collection of materials, resources, and professional development. In this way, they are creating their own specialized backpack for their particular teaching situation. I emphasize that at the crux of surviving the teaching profession, and more importantly to thrive as a teacher, we must realize that our classrooms are very special, unique places where generalizations don't work. We must, of course, follow the curriculum map. We must, of course, work within our department or grade level to reach goals that are set by administrators.

However, years ago, one of my mentors shared a quote that has stuck with me, constantly helping me recalibrate my teaching over the years. Neil Postman said, "Once you have learned to ask questions – relevant and appropriate and substantial questions – you have learned how to learn and no one can keep you from learning whatever you want or need to know." This quote has guided me to ask, over and over again, to ask myself what do these particular kiddos need to get from point A to point Z and all the stops in between? In essence, I'm constantly looking for what to throw in my battered backpack to help them become the best versions of themselves—students who have the skills, confidence, social and emotional skills, and intellectual curiosity to follow their passions.

The tour guide

When I become overwhelmed, or one of my own children, or my students at school feel paralyzed with what to do next, I begin to plan like Dora the Explorer. Dora simply followed steps sequentially with a goal in mind to reach a certain destination. The key? You have to know the "certain destination." In teaching, the day-to-day stuff can start to feel insurmountable, so it is crucial that you begin with the end in mind, as Franklin Covey would say. What does this look like in practical terms?

First, sit down with the standards you need to assess. From those, choose a few that are the "power standards" that you believe will be most beneficial for your students. Then, create a final test. The final test should reflect everything you believe that your students should know and be able to do at the end of the particular unit. For example, I just finished a unit on analytic paragraph writing with my 8th graders. The goal of the unit was that my students would be able to analyze a specific literary device in two complete paragraphs, correctly using citations from the text, in 38 minutes (our class period). I created a test that simply said: **Using your independent reading novel, analyze the author's characterization of the protagonist**.

I knew that they'd have to be able to:

1) Use complete sentences
2) Know literary techniques and how to discuss them
3) Have the stamina to write for 38 minutes
4) Read an entire book
5) Incorporate citations correctly

Once I created the test and broke it down into the components, I had to figure out what my first steps were. I know my students really well by now, in February, and I knew where they were struggling based on their recent essay. However, if I didn't, I'd give them the exact same task as a pre-assessment, but switch it up to be about a book we'd read together. This would allow me to see the raw materials that I was working with. With this group, I knew that they didn't have the stamina and automaticity to be successful in high school which is more rigorous and less spoon-fed than the middle school.

I'll break down my unit from the planning perspective for you here. First, I'd need to book some time in the library for my students to pick out books. In other years, I'd have simply told them to bring in an independent reading book, but coming out of the Covid years, I wasn't sure they'd have a good idea of how to do this. Always give yourself more time than you think necessary. I expected to use one day, but I booked two. Sure enough, there were many kids who were absent on the first day, and a few who couldn't choose. This step was crucial though. I needed my students to like what they were reading in order to get them through this exercise in independently reading and responding to literature. I knew they needed this skill since I have a son who is a freshman who was currently doing just that.

Once everyone had their book, I needed to teach them how to divide their book into chunks. We were going to have 16 reading days and 8 writing days. I don't assign homework, so they were going to read one day, write a journal, then read another day or two, then respond with a journal. Once students divided it up, I showed them how to write in their agenda when to do the task. This is crucial—they shouldn't write Chapters 1–4 due on the due date. They needed to plan backwards themselves. They needed to write which chapters to read leading up to the due date. For example, if they needed to have Chapters 1–4 due on Friday, they had to look at our schedule and see that we had only two reading days, therefore reading two chapters on each date. If they were to write "Chapters 1–4 due" on Friday, they would not have taken the important task of delineating when the work gets done.

New teachers can fall into this same trap, so when you are planning, break the tasks down into what can be accomplished in one class period, and make room for what you need to circle back to. I knew, without a doubt, that I'd need to constantly do mini-lessons on complete sentences and citations. Most would be able to pick up on the literary devices, and most would eventually gain the stamina from our repeated practice throughout the month, but years of experience have told me that sentences and citations will always need multiple reinforcements. If you aren't sure what power standards you should focus on or if you aren't aware of the areas that will be bumpy, ask another teacher who teaches the same grade or a similar unit. They will surely know, and teachers love to share this kind of knowledge.

After you have broken down what you need to teach each day, make sure you get clear in your thinking on what the kiddos need to do each day as well. Too often, we can get so caught up in what we have to do that we forget that the real learning isn't going to come from our direct instruction, but more so from students' own experiences and our guidance during their struggle. Think like a student. What do you need to do to make the learning engaging? How can we improve our kiddos experiences in the classroom? When I have material that is either inherently dry or challenging, I make sure there's lots of choice involved, which is why we did this unit with an independent novel of their choosing. Keep in mind the attention span of the kiddos in your age group as well.

As you read through all of these considerations in planning, you might be feeling overwhelmed, and that is never going to go away. You are attempting to do something absolutely insane! You have a room of 25 individual students who have all reached different levels of mastery, and you are tasked with creating units and lessons that are engaging, rigorous, differentiated, and once you get comfortable, the goalposts will change. This is the nature of education, and you are the only one who can guard the students' experience in the classroom by planning for solid instruction that is developmentally appropriate and takes into account who they are as little humans.

So, what did I do to make my admittedly dry unit work? I allowed them plenty of brain breaks. I started classes with funny videos or inspiring ones. I allowed them to listen to their novel instead of just reading it. I allowed them to read the same book as their BFF. I asked them to complete check-in's with me, and if they hated their book they could get a new one. We did many book talks where they were able to socialize and talk about their book. There were eight journals required (see Figure 6.1), but they were allowed to skip one with no penalty. Their journals where they were getting all the feedback on their writing were very low stakes class work grades (20% of their overall average) and I provided fun Blookets, EdPuzzles, and Quizlet reviews for their quizzes (accounting for 30% of their grade) on the more rote memorization material like definitions of literary terms. Any time you can gamify "boring" material, the better. By the time we got to their test day, when they had to write only ONE perfect paragraph, they had reached automaticity and were almost bored with the task. *When teaching is scaffolded like this, and students see an end in sight, final assessments become non-events, as they already know they can do the task well.*

One of the keys to mapmaking (planning), is to understand the pacing, and to give yourself and your students plenty of room for growth and grace. Things will happen. I live in Buffalo. We have snow days. We've all had to learn to deal with fluctuation in attendance. There's going to be an assembly, or you're going to have to go to a meeting. Make sure that the pace you are prescribing for the unit is one that allows joy in the journey for both you and your students. However, a huge word of caution here: don't plan units that won't sustain themselves. I'm a part of education chats on social media, and time and time again, I read about teachers, new and veterans, who are stuck with a unit that has lost its steam. I tend to take a month for a novel, with students reading and doing activities throughout. I do lots of mini-lessons and provide for practice. There's a fine balance between students getting into the rhythm of the unit and them growing bored.

Over the years, I've learned a few tricks. No one ever explained these types of things to me, and frankly, my life would have been much easier if I'd received this type of common sense, practical advice. I hope these tricks can give you a leg up!

1. Give yourself time at the beginning of the unit and at the end. I build in two days to introduce the unit because I want to make sure that I can plan a great hook activity. I build in two days at the end for "test review." I never use both days, but I can bump everything back if needed.

2. I always make my tests on Thursday because Fridays are when many of my athletes disappear early for tournaments. If there's a quiet task, I always do that on Mondays, as I want to have a few minutes to reconnect with kiddos after the weekend. Some kiddos really need you to be their touchstone, and a quiet Monday allows for those interactions.

3. I write the schedule of what we will be doing in class and what is due that day on the board for the entire week. It looks like this:
   Monday: Chapter 1 is due/we will have a quiz in class
   Tuesday: journal 1 is due/we will be reading in class

Wednesday: nothing due/learning about characterization

Thursday: Chapters 1–4 is due/we will review complete sentences

Friday: we will be circling up today to talk about protagonists

4. Sharing what the day will "feel like" helps with behavior management. When they know the expectation for the kind of learning that will be happening, they are more able to process the way they should behave.

5. When students are absent, I take a picture of the board and send it to them. Then, they know both what they have to do and what they missed. As an aside, I think the schools who require teachers to post objectives on the board each day aren't wrong, but they often go about it in the wrong way. Knowing what to expect each day is important when creating a classroom community, but I don't know any students or adults who likes to be spoken to or about the way most objectives are written.

Finally, there are two "tricks of the trade" that many might disagree with. If you are bombing a lesson, or in the worst scenario, an entire unit, then absolve yourself and quit. Sit down with your students and ask them what went wrong. I've done this a half dozen times in my career, and the reason something was failing is rarely what I thought. I tried teaching *Farewell to Manzanar,* a book about Japanese internment camps, without giving it enough context, so my 7th grade students were perpetually confused. They didn't understand that this book happened in the United States, and when we talked through this, they were suddenly much more interested, and we completed the book together with lots of their input. Another time, when I was teaching Juniors, my enthusiasm for Walt Whitman wasn't the least bit contagious. I chose to give up and ask for help, and students ended up researching poets from the same time period and we did a poetry battle instead, using the poems from their poets. It turned into one of my most memorable lessons because it was co-created

with my students. I don't recommend you quit every time something is shakey, but it isn't the end of the world.

So here's the second secret. Watch the movies. Go ahead. Pop
some popcorn, make crockpot hot chocolate, encourage them to
flop on the floor. They don't have to be silent either. Just quiet.
Giggling and fun are fully permitted. If they want to dress up on
movie day, let them. If they want to wear pajamas, get permission from your administration, but encourage it. Wear pajamas
too. You don't have to do compare/contrast assignments because
your students will naturally critically compare them. You can
read more about how to utilize movies for SEL in my book,
Movie Magic, but it is essential to allow joy in your classroom,
and movies do that.

Celebration circles

Like watching the movie, celebrations aren't always appreciated,
but celebrations are crucial for classroom communities. To return
to my Dora analogy, it is no accident that when they reach their
destination, they celebrate: "We did it/We did it/We did it/Lo
hicimos!" The important takeaway here isn't that Dora made it,
but that the entire group made it *together*. This is the same for
your classroom. Again, think of your kiddos as your tour group.
They all have to get to the destination, one way or another, or
you haven't done your job. Some students are going to require
more time, and that's ok. I allow more time by extremely flexible
due dates as well as support from my co-teacher. I don't take off
points for late work, as some people just need more time.

However, this is not an effective practice unless you help
those who are falling behind. If they are lost, going down the
wrong path, or missing the supplies or tools to get where we
are going, I don't just leave them to their own devices! Instead,
I pull students aside and ask what's going on, how I can help,
and jot down on a sticky note a plan we devise together. Usually,
that plan is simply a list, but many times it includes a support
that they may not have asked for in front of everyone else. For
example, during this past unit, I had a young lady who left her

book at her grandma's house, and she couldn't get it until the weekend. As an adult, it was easy for me to see that she should simply go to the library and see if our librarian could get her an extra copy. This idea had never occurred to her, but she was so grateful that she caught herself up that night.

During this same unit, a young man was missing several journals, though he appeared to be working in class. After some investigation on my part, I figured out he knew how to scramble our student monitoring system, GoGuardian, and make it appear he was in Google Classroom by using DuckDuckGo, an app that creates private browsing. I pulled him into the hall, complimented his incognito, ninja-like avoidance of my work, but explained that if he was ever going to get a good job using his superpowers for good, he'd need to know how to write quality paragraphs. I warned him that I was on to him, called his dad for an in-depth conversation about the implications of his computer knowledge, and then offered him an extension on the paragraphs. I went into our GoGuardian settings and blocked DuckDuckGo, and set this student's parameters much tighter.

You might be wondering why I didn't punish him in any tangible way. First, I'd remind you that being a middle school boy whose teacher is having this conversation is punishment in itself. Having the same teacher talk to your dad about your browsing habits, is torture. Finally, I take a broad view of behavior and my role in correcting it. Did he do something wrong? Yes. Was it hurting anyone other than himself? No. Could I coerce him to learn what I needed him to learn? Yes, his dad took his phone and computer until he was caught up. Would writing a referral, involving another adult to see him in a negative light, be beneficial? In other words, would giving this kiddo a non-related punishment like lunch detention improve my relationship with him or move the needle in the direction I wanted it to go? No, definitely not. I erred on the side of the kiddo. Am I ever wrong? Do I ever seem like the fool who believed a kiddo would change or learn from a situation, only to face the same issues again? Yep. But, I still err on the side of the child who doesn't have impulse control mastered, whose hormonal roller coaster is dizzying, and I'll take another route with them the next time.

Designing assignments that are attainable for all students is tricky. I want the destination to be worth the trip for all of us, but I have to keep in mind the limitations of some, and the strengths of others. I consider the destination to be the top of a mountain. Each student might have a different path to the top, and it's my job as their teacher to help map it out for them. If a student can easily do the work, I'd make sure they have ample challenges added. For instance, students who already knew how to write good paragraphs were emailed videos on how to use semicolons, given an interactive quiz on the skill, and then challenged to use a semicolon in their next journal entry. New teachers sometimes feel like they can't provide this kind of non-graded side work for students, but the ones who were bored with the journey need this type of differentiation. I had some students who read two books during this unit. I had one who read three! I had some students who were reading graphic novels, and I challenged a select few big readers to compare the development of their protagonist with the protagonist in *The Outsiders*, the novel we'd just completed.

Remember my test, the one that reflected my final destination for students: **Using your independent reading novel, analyze the author's characterization of the protagonist.** All my students made it to the top. We all reached this destination, but their journey had required Backpacks that were suited just for them. As the Tour Guide I provided tools and scaffolding, as well as side challenges, but on test day, students were given this same task. The range of paragraphs I received reflected the abilities of my students, but I was able to use the same Single Point Rubric (Table 6.1) to measure their progress.

Let me interrupt here with a word about rubrics. You need them! The best way to set attainable and rigorous goals for your students is to create a rubric that clearly lays out what success looks like. Pro tip: if you ever struggle to create a rubric, your assignment is probably too "all over the place" or unclear in its purpose. Remember, rubrics don't have to cover every single aspect of the assignment, but if you are measuring it as a part of the grade, it should show up on the rubric. The Single Point Rubric is awesome because it allows me—and my students—to focus on what I'm looking for. If they go above and beyond, I can

TABLE 6.1 Single Point Paragraph Rubric

Almost there!	Achieved our goal!	Woo hoo!
	The response is a complete paragraph of at least six sentences with a topic sentence that includes the author and the title of the book.	
	The response uses specific examples from the book to analyze how the author characterizes the protagonist. There are two different examples provided with evidence from the text, correctly cited, with pages numbers.	
	75% of the sentences are complete and grammatically correct.	
	75% of the capitalization is correct	
	The student's "voice" is evident and the response engages with the book in an authentic way. The student has clearly read the book, rather than a summary.	

take note of it. If they haven't met the mark, I have space to provide advice to them.

Once you've arrived at the destination—in this case, a well-developed analysis paragraph requiring citations to support their point—everyone should celebrate. Celebrations though are not reserved for only those who met every requirement or criteria on the rubric. Celebrations are for the collective "we" of your class, an official ending to a unit that your classroom community conquered together. These don't have to be parties, and certainly can't be all the time, but there must be official notice that the group has moved forward together. For this unit, I had students compare their first journal entry to their final paragraph. We dissected what they did better. They were excited to tell me that they italicized the title of a book. Other students pointed out that they finally knew how to do the citations correctly. I pointed out that they were actually using two different pieces of evidence instead of saying the same thing twice.

I try to do these celebration conversations in a circle. It isn't just academic, and students need to understand the social and emotional skills that are required to "do school." In this particular unit, I had watched many of my higher students struggle when challenged, and some of those who usually struggle were cajoled to keep moving forward, even if they didn't want to. This had been a tremendous amount of reading and writing for students post pandemic. In our circle, we asked all students to "whip around" the circle identifying what they were most proud of learning. All students were able to identify significant progress, and now, the students of room 255 will write complete paragraphs every time. They can now approach their high school assignments with the confidence that they know how to write quality paragraphs. Importantly, if they forget something, they have 110 other students who they know made a similar journey, and they can ask for help.

Celebrations will look different, depending on the grade level, but I highly recommend the celebration circle. Point out the SEL competencies that your students have mastered. I explained to my students that they'd really come to understand Self-Management since they'd had to organize their time and chunk the book. We shared our bright spots and our "oops" moments. We had lollipops and talked about our month together with this unit. Interestingly, both the students I mentioned before acknowledged their situation. The girl whose book was at her grandma's house mentioned that she was thankful that the librarian had helped her out. The boy who was a ninja at avoiding work talked about how hard it had been to catch up when he fell behind. As a new teacher, you'll be tempted to skip these celebrations, but please, do yourself a favor, and make the time. You need these celebration circles as much as they do.

If you are worried about how a celebration circle might look to an administrator, consider this: invite your principal or department chair in. Does that sound nuts to you? It is, a little. But, it is how you grow too. When you provide a path to the top of the mountain for all students, and they arrive, they will be plenty happy to talk about it and reflect. Metacognition is an extremely difficult concept to grasp because it is so abstract, but celebrations allow students to think about their own thinking! Ask your mentor, department chair, or administrator, and especially families to come observe a celebration circle. Post student work in a gallery walk for those who stop into your room. Help others see the view you are providing your students!

This chapter has been a bit different from the rest of the book, but I thought it was important to zoom out a little and see how the practical considerations like "plan a standards based final assessment" and "provide scaffolding" and "communicate with families as partners in their child's education" actually looks. I began this chapter by acknowledging that there are so many times in teaching when we have this seemingly never-ending list of things we are supposed to be doing without really talking about the *how*.

That's because the *how* is the art of teaching, the part that is what makes our profession magical. We each bring to our classrooms a unique set of skills and talents. Our personalities are inescapable, and no matter how hard you try, you will be you in the classroom, so there's no use pretending to be someone you are not. I'm not funny, at least on purpose, yet I see hilarious teachers reach students. Does that mean I will fail? No, I won't because I bring my own Backpack with deep content knowledge, a love of literature, a broad view of where my students are going, and a "mom" persona that makes my 8th grade students, my college students, and my mentees feel that they are loved and supported. Imagine if I tried to stifle all of that and try to be funny instead. I'd fail, and I'd deprive my students of the unique experience I create for them in our classroom community. The great part about planning like Dora the Explorer is that you get to bring your own special brand to your classroom. Use the Mentoring Moment questions to help create memorable journeys for your students.

Mentoring moment

1. Where will you find the "map" of what you need to be teaching? Try to identify the "power standards" or emphasized skills. A good way to determine a school or department's goals for students is to look at what skills or competencies are spiraled into the curriculum. What did you notice?

2. What lessons or units do you want to incorporate that will fit into the overall goals for students? Is there wiggle room? If your school provides a more scripted curriculum, determine where there are spaces for your creativity.

3. What tools or resources can you provide for your special education students? Gifted students? Those with social or emotional difficulties? How can you help fill their backpack with goodies to help them on their journey?

4. What special skills or talents do you have in your backpack? How can you incorporate your interests into the curriculum? Remember, it is easier to be the most amazing version of yourself as a teacher when you are authentic and allow your passions to shine through.

5. What are your thoughts about celebration circles? If this sounds like you, what would you do to make them special? Be imaginative and remember that students love novelty and don't mind a bit that you are silly or sentimental. If you don't think celebration circles are for you, don't force it. How can you achieve the same level of reflection and metacognition with a different culminating activity? Be yourself as you plan a celebration that you can truly get behind.

7

Ask me anything

I love advice columns. Dear Abby, of course. But, I have also loved those in *Teen Beat*, *Tiger Beat*, *Teen*, and *Mademoiselle* magazines. Heck, I'll read the "Garden Corner" advice column in the local paper, even though I don't own a trowel or even have a watering can. As you might imagine, as a connoisseur of advice columns, I've been anxiously awaiting the writing of this chapter. I wanted to come up with a catchy title, like I have my own column, but "Ask Me Anything" does the job. In this final chapter, I'm going to share with you some of the questions mentees have asked me over the years, and more recently, some of the questions I received from social media. There's a catch though, that I had not foreseen, but hit me just today. I have to answer each question from three different viewpoints! What I mean by this, is that the answer to each question will differ if it is from me, the Mentor; or me, the Union President; or me, your Work Mom. You'll see. This is going to be interesting!

Can I date a coworker?

> MENTOR: I'm pretty sure that most schools don't have a rule forbidding dating unless it involves a power dynamic, like you can't date the principal. You wouldn't want to do that for so many reasons, but at the top of the list is that they are likely very old compared to you! So, yeah, let me check our contract to see if there's anything in it. I know that they look at new teachers pretty closely, so

DOI: 10.4324/9781003365921-7

I wouldn't want to draw too much attention to myself. Dating a coworker will make you the center of the rumor mill. I'll check the rules for you.

UNION PRESIDENT: I'm happy that you are considering the implications of dating in the workplace. While your Mentor is correct, there is nothing against it in the contract, per se, I'd advise you against it. Remember that as a new teacher you are under the microscope, and you want the people who are looking that intently at you to see only you, not you connected to someone else. Also, which building do you teach in? It is probably viewed differently in elementary, middle, and high school. Problematic. That's my word for this: problematic. Not illegal or unethical, but definitely problematic. Being a new teacher is hard enough without adding an entire other element. **However, when it comes to contractual issues, every teacher needs to remember that all contracts are different and you have to check yours to see the rules!**

WORK MOM: Oooh! Who do you have in mind? This one is complicated. Lots of people do meet their significant other at work. Is this an attraction or do you think you "like/like" them? I mean, I'd hate to see you miss this opportunity if you are really into them. Also, lots of teachers marry other teachers. If you are thinking that this might just be an attraction, don't risk it. Imagine if you have a horrible date and then you have to look at them every day for the rest of your life? Hmmm… ok. If it is attraction, I'm a no, for sure. If you genuinely think there's something there, I'd go for it, but do not, I repeat, do not, bring it into school. You'll need to be very discreet. No social media. No walking in together, that kind of thing. I trust you. How exciting!

I really have to go to the bathroom. What do I do?

MENTOR: Look around for someone in the hall to watch your kiddos for a minute. It can be pretty much anyone who works for the school, but preferably a teacher, or teacher's aid. You can call the office and ask them to send someone to cover for you. Don't leave them alone unless you are going to explode from one end or the other. It's a liability. You can ask a nearby teacher to keep an ear out too. Call my room or text me, and I'll find someone for you.

UNION PRESIDENT: Don't leave your students alone. It can be considered negligence, and you can lose your job immediately. Something terrible can happen while you are gone, and you'll find the fault lies on your shoulders. If anyone reports that your students were alone, I'd be in a disciplinary meeting with you. I'm serious. If you are going to puke, take the wastebasket and puke in the hallway. Then, call the nurse. To be honest, drink less coffee. Leaving your kiddos is not allowed.

WORK MOM: I've been there. I almost peed my pants on the daily when I was pregnant. Find out who has a co-teacher in a classroom near you. Then, if you have an emergency, you can call their room and one of them will come over. You'll find your work friends and won't have to worry. In the meantime, have you met the secretary? She's my go-to for anything. She can get someone to your room immediately. She drinks green tea with honey, and I buy her one every time I go through the drive thru. She's saved me more times than you'd imagine.

I lost my temper with a student. What do I do? It was bad

MENTOR: Define bad. You might think something is worse than it actually is. If you raised your voice, don't worry about it too much. If you swore at a student or said something mean, you are going to need to weigh out whether to contact their parents or not. Some kiddos go home and report everything, but others don't say a word. The most important thing right now is to consider how to repair your relationship with the child. Reach out to the kiddo's guidance counselor. He does restorative practices and could mediate the situation if you wanted. It really depends. If you didn't swear or call the student a name or anything, you are probably fine. We are only human.

UNION PRESIDENT: Have you had a history with this child in terms of behavior? If not, what caused the situation to escalate so quickly? If so, do you have a paper trail of communication with the family or interventions you've tried? Does the child have a behavior plan? Take a look at the child's behavior tab in the management system. Does this child have a history? If so, you probably aren't even a blip on the radar. If not, you may have crossed a line that will end up with a phone call about you to the principal. What exactly happened? If you just raised just write it down so that you have it if you need it. I'd lie low for a few days, and treat the child neutrally. It's ok to apologize for losing your temper, but don't get into details with the child or anyone else. Don't talk to anyone about this. It sounds like you raised your voice and that's it. Not the worst thing in the world.

WORK MOM: Oh no! Everyone loses it sometimes, so don't beat yourself up too much. What happened? Tell me exactly. Ok. So you just raised your voice and said you were very disappointed in him. You made him log off the computer and put his head down and said it was a shame he couldn't behave well enough to earn rewards and that if he didn't improve his behavior he'd be spending Field Day in the principal's office. Ok. Hmm. Did you say he disappointed you or did you call him a disappointment? Just that he disappointed you. Well, I think that you are most upset because this isn't like you, but I think you just need to apologize to the kiddo. Just tell him the truth. You are human. You were tired. He made you feel like you weren't doing a good job, and you wish you had thought before you spoke. That's it. Doesn't sound too bad. Let's get coffee after school.

How do I ever finish all this grading?

MENTOR: It gets easier. Are you grading everything you assign? Definitely don't do that! When they are practicing a skill, you can check that they are finishing it and provide on-the-spot feedback, but you don't need to give everything a number for the gradebook. Are you utilizing programs that do the grading for you? Try EdPuzzle. It's free and self-grading. You should also be using Google Forms for your quizzes because you can lock their computer to prevent cheating, but it also "talks to" our learning management system, so you don't have to enter grades, you just upload them. I'll show you how to do that. It's a lifesaver.

UNION PRESIDENT: Contractually, we have to have two grades in the portal per week. Are you doing that? Make sure that you have at least four quizzes and two tests each quarter. That's not in writing anywhere, but that's what we've kind of decided is the best idea. Don't get tempted into buying lesson plans or materials. The Superintendent was notified of a teacher using materials they'd bought that said "for classroom use only." Turns out, the fine print said it couldn't be posted digitally, and the teacher missed that. A mom of some kid saw it. Turns out she's a copyright lawyer. Tough break right there. Anyway, just make sure you stick to the rules. Ask someone in your department if you aren't sure.

WORK MOM: I'm going to be totally honest with you, and I don't want to depress you or steal your passion. The fact is though, this job will take all of your time. There's always more to do. More grading. More committees. More lessons to plan. More professional development opportunities. There are seasons for all of this, and you are in the spring of things. Popping with new ideas, budding into a school leader, and helping young minds grow. There's nothing better. However, you have to create boundaries for yourself or you'll burn out. So many people do. When I was your age, I assigned way too much and graded all the time. I learned to allow kiddos to practice without grading it. We do things in class that I can assess as they happen. I take notes on my clipboard about what I see. Your boundaries will change, and you can move the line, but for now, you have your physical and mental health to worry about. Teaching all day, going to graduate classes until 8:00 two nights a week, and grading everything is going to make you physically sick and drain your mental reserves. Next week, grade two things, like you have to, and the rest is for practice. Those things you assign—use a rubric. Don't invent the wheel. There's free stuff online too.

I feel like I'm going crazy. How do you handle all the nonsense with these kids?

MENTOR: The bad news is, there's always nonsense. We have to say things like, "Please take the markers out of your ears." It seems antithetical to learning to have all this chaos of kids being kids, but the good news is, learning thrives in laughter. Don't be so serious. You can be the teacher and also put markers in your ears right back. Some new teachers fear losing control when there is a goofy vibe, but if you always let kiddos know what is appropriate for the situation, try to make the nonsense a part of your day.

UNION PRESIDENT: Safety. Safety. Safety. You need to make sure that your class is a safe learning environment physically and socially and emotionally. Don't let the goofiness become dangerous. If they are being appropriate, it's good to have a light environment, but the number one reason I sit in meetings with new teachers is that their classroom management is bad and something happens that causes an injury or the joking went too far. I think it's good to stay more authoritative in the beginning of your career. Save the goofy stuff for people who are on more solid ground.

WORK MOM: Just wait until you have your own kiddos. It's like a second shift at home. You just have to laugh. Commiserate with your grade level or team. Your work friends are the only ones who are going to understand a story that begins, "It was Friday the 13th, the week of Homecoming, and the cafeteria was serving those giant pizza sized chocolate chip cookies. Let me tell you what happened in 8th period." There's nothing better than your work family. We get it. Now tell me, what's going on now?

What are the rules I'm actually supposed to enforce?

MENTOR: This is a tough one. Each administration we have of higher ups has an agenda that they care about more out of the handbook. Last principal was dead set that phones were going to stay in lockers. This principal doesn't think phones are a problem in the hallways, but students' attitudes need adjusting. You kind of have to roll with it. If you have lunch duty, bus duty, or hall duty, ask someone what to look out for. Which battles are you supposed to be fighting? Ask me if you aren't sure. Don't go around writing referrals though. Lots of admin look at that as a weakness in the new teachers. Just check with me if you really aren't sure.

UNION PRESIDENT: You want to be careful to follow the guidelines that the administrators gave you. If they didn't give you anything specific, take the lead from someone who has been doing this for years. You don't want to get tangled up in things that are out of your control anyway. It's tricky to enforce rules or discipline students you don't know, so I'd leave that to the veterans, at least at first. Follow directives, but be careful of causing yourself problems.

WORK MOM: Do what you are required, but lay low. It is really hard for new teachers to establish authority in their own rooms, much less in a cafeteria full of hyped up kiddos. You want most of your interactions to be positive with students in the school, so look for the good and focus on that. There's always those teachers who will jump on the behavior kids, so you let them take that route. Look for the kiddo who needs a caring adult to say hi, and spend your time there.

All of my teacher friend's classrooms are Pinterest perfect and Instagram ready. Mine is boring. Should I be worried?

MENTOR: It's not a contest. Don't give it another thought. Make your room look inviting. Busy, messy classrooms are the best places to learn, not a room that looks too orderly to breathe.

UNION PRESIDENT: 50% of the crap you see online is against all kinds of fire codes, school rules, and makes new teachers seem like they are just playing school. Teach the kiddos and you'll be fine.

WORK MOM: You know what I say, right? "Comparison is the thief of joy." Actually, I say that, but it is definitely a quote from Theodore Roosevelt. I'm really concerned by the culture of perfection that is being put out there about teaching. Teaching is wild. Your room will be a mess. Kiddos will spill things. Your carpets will have weird stains. But, you bring the light into the place. Just do that and forget Pinterest and Instagram.

Should I go to school board meetings?

MENTOR: Go to any meeting that involves you. Otherwise, it isn't necessary. However, I'd read the Board minutes to keep an eye on what's going on in the district. If anything big is happening, it goes through them first.

UNION PRESIDENT: Definitely go to the meeting where you are hired, receive tenure, or any other recognition. It's not required by any means, but you can learn a lot about the district, its politics, and the members of the community by going to the meetings.

WORK MOM: Just when you have to. They start at 7:00 and go for hours. You can always watch them on YouTube when they are posted. But, yes, you have to go to the ones that involve you. Otherwise, I'd steer clear of Board stuff. It's very political.

I really don't like the teachers or administrators here. What should I do?

MENTOR: Have you really given everyone a chance? Have you let anyone get to know you besides me? Do you socialize at all? I know you are busy with the "work of work," but you have to find time for the special moments of teaching too. Take a walk around right after the students leave. You'll see little clusters of tired teachers all over the place. Just say hello. Smile. Give it a try for the rest of the year, maybe two. The first year, it is hard to know much of anything.

UNION PRESIDENT: Your mentor probably isn't going to like that I say this, but I'd start looking for another job. Unhappy, disconnected educators cause themselves problems. If you aren't invested, and don't want to be a part of this particular school family that doesn't mean you won't make a good teacher somewhere else. However, I've had to help teachers resign from positions instead of being fired because they let their misery with the school lead to bad decisions or they simply dropped the ball. Better to retain your reputation and control of the situation then wait for it to implode. Disliking the teachers and the administrators is a bad sign.

WORK MOM: I'm sorry this is happening to you. It's very overwhelming. I'd say that you need to keep your eye on other openings both within our district and in other districts. I love having you teach here, but there's no reason to make yourself miserable, especially during a teacher shortage. You have other opportunities. If you think the vibe is off, you are probably off, and if you feel this way about the other teachers and administrators, they probably know it. This dynamic will never work.

What's the worst thing that ever happened to you at school?

MENTOR: I cried in front of my AP Literature students. It was because I was very tired from staying up grading their papers, and I was writing my own for my Master's class as well. One of the girls rolled her eyes when I had tried to say something clever. I don't even know what it was, but immediately I was back in high school on the other side of the podium, back in the land of the mean girls. The class went dead silent, and the worst part was that one of the nice kids went and got my department chair. It was truly awful, but I'm here to tell the tale, so you know, you survive.

UNION PRESIDENT: It didn't happen to me, but a student teacher. He had a bad lesson, no doubt. Me and my department chair had been in the room to take notes, and it bombed. When the kiddos left, he said, "I don't want to be a teacher. I hated every minute of that," and he walked out. We never saw him again. We tried to get him back, and I even went to his address and left a message taped to his apartment. It was heartbreaking to see this talented guy give up because he felt like a failure. He wasn't a failure, his lesson was. Lessons can be fixed.

WORK MOM: Umm... probably that one time when I was walking up the stairs and a student behind me stepped on the back of my dress and ripped it. It was a hippy kind of dress that had a tighter top connected to a flowy bottom. The flowy bottom was hanging by a few threads, but my granny panties were on full display. I grabbed the bottom of my dress and ran to the nurse who promptly safety-pinned my dress back together, and I was only a little late for my class. Unfortunately, they all knew why. But, sometimes, you just have to laugh, and I did.

As this chapter comes to a close, I think it is important to note that I am Mentor, Union President, and Work Mom all rolled up into one. As you read, sometimes those roles are in conflict with each other. Like me, you are going to find times where your roles will be at odds with one another. Try being a teacher, a coach, a daughter, a wife, and a mother. Try being a teacher, graduate student, husband, and brother. These roles will collide, and you will need to decide which hat you need to wear to best serve the students in front of you. Changing lives is the most amazing feeling in the world, and teachers do it all the time. We have this incredible opportunity to be "that person" for students who absolutely need a caring adult to fuel their confidence and even sometimes their will to live. This is not a job to be taken lightly, but a calling to protect. Use your mentors, find your teacher family, and you will thrive!

Now that you have read my multi-tiered answers to this chapter's questions, it's time for the Mentoring Moment. In this ending exercise, discuss each question with your mentor and share your thoughts as well.

Mentoring moment

1. Should you date a coworker?
2. What can you do to prepare for the inevitability of REALLY needing to go to the bathroom? Who do I know who can help me?
3. What should I do if I lose my temper with a student? Is there a way to prevent that from happening? When should I call home?
4. How do I manage the grading? Can I cut back? What are the expectations for my district in terms of the number of assignments per week, and the number that are required at the end of the quarter? Can I use a rubric? Do I have to grade everything?
5. What kind of nonsense drives me crazy? Do I need to control it or laugh it off? Am I managing my classroom well? Am I handling the physical, social, and emotional safety of my students well? What can I do to create the right vibe?

6. What rules are there within my assigned duties that I need to enforce? Which infractions should I perhaps leave to others? How might I address issues with students I don't know? Is there a way to connect with students within my assigned duties?

7. What do I think a "good" classroom looks like? What kind of learning environment do I think is best for my subject area, age group, and my personality?

8. Should I attend a school board meeting? What might I learn?

9. Am I giving the people in this building a chance to become my work family? If not, what is holding me back? Is there something I should be doing? Or, should I start looking for a new job?

10. What's the worst thing I've ever had happen to me in the classroom? How do I feel about it now?

Afterword

I'm feeling a little old. This book came to be because of conversations I was having with Nicole Coolican, a full-grown adult lady, my mentee. We determined that I am old enough to be her mother. I could be older than her mother, but I didn't want to know. She soon began calling me her Work Mom, and I love it. I'm not feeling old for all of the normal reasons, though they exist too. My one knee is kinda off, and I have whole social media platforms that I don't care to understand. I did accidentally think that this April I'd be turning 50, but as it turns out, it isn't until 2024. Nope, not those old people things. Something different.

I'm feeling a little old because I am now, undeniably, in the second half of my career as a teacher, and probably, the final third. This, in itself, doesn't make me feel especially old either, though please have an intervention if I start counting down the years. No, I still love teaching, can't imagine not going to school every September, and I am plenty feisty to keep people on their toes. If anything, I've given myself permission to be more protective and loud about the things that matter most to me: my students, their mental health, and the need to protect public education.

The thing that makes me feel old is that I have lived so much of my life in education that I am starting to feel the ebbs and flows, the tides shifting and changing, always. When I first started teaching, Mary Potter, one of my excellent mentors, taught me a very important lesson that I've been absorbing more and more each year. She delivered this particular piece of wisdom after a morning of intense Professional Development, and she was remarkably calm, I thought, for we had just been delivered some "new" thing we were expected to do. We went for a drive along the ocean to get a coffee, vent, and chain smoke (because, back then, it wasn't something you didn't do) on our lunch break. I was babbling my worries to her, and she listened patiently.

But then, she pulled over along the water, and turned and looked at me. I don't remember her exact words, so I'll give you the gist of what she said:

> I've been teaching for twenty years, and you don't have to worry. New people will come along every few years, and each administration will have different agendas and initiatives. You are a good teacher, and experience will make you great. Listen to everyone, but follow your own way. You are the only one who can make your classroom a magical place. No one else.

Those words have stuck with me, and now, after I myself have been teaching for over 20 years, I know Mary is right. I've said the same thing, more or less, minus the chain smoking, to Nicole and all of the other teachers I've mentored through the years. We all bring our own brand of magic to our classrooms, and I'm convinced that is how public education will survive, and even thrive at times. Each generation brings ideas, theories, and perspectives that the generation before could never have fathomed. If you were to have told me about current educational problems, I literally could not have comprehended them, and the future will bring new quandaries for the current new teachers.

Being open to the advice and guidance of veteran ("old") teachers is important, but it should be balanced with what *you* have experienced with teaching and learning. That's my hope as you begin a career that has shaped my entire life, one that I adore and struggle with constantly. Consult the Map, grab your Backpack, find your work family, and share the magic that is uniquely yours! This book is meant to be another voice in your ear, a mentoring mom voice, but it is truly my hope that you do as Mary told me: "Listen to everyone, but follow your own way."

For Product Safety Concerns and Information please contact our
EU representative GPSR@taylorandfrancis.com Taylor & Francis
Verlag GmbH, Kaufingerstraße 24, 80331 München, Germany